VOLUME 5

FIRST and SECOND SAMUEL

Frank Johnson

ABINGDON PRESS
Nashville

FIRST AND SECOND SAMUEL

Copyright © 1988 by Graded Press

This book is printed on recycled, acid-free paper.

Library of Congress Cataloging-in-Publication Data

Cokesbury basic Bible commentary.
    Basic Bible commentary/by Linda B. Hinton . . .[et al.].
      p. cm.
    Originally published: Cokesbury basic Bible commentary. Nashville: Graded Press. c1988.
    ISBN 0-687-02620-2 (pbk.: v. 1: alk. paper)
    1. Bible—Commentaries.   I. Hinton, Linda B.   II. Title.
[BS491.2.C65   1994]
220.7—dc20

94-10965
CIP

ISBN 0-687-02624-5 (v. 5, 1–2 Samuel)
ISBN 0-687-02620-2 (v. 1, Genesis)
ISBN 0-687-02621-0 (v. 2, Exodus–Leviticus)
ISBN 0-687-02622-9 (v. 3, Numbers–Deuteronomy)
ISBN 0-687-02623-7 (v. 4, Joshua–Ruth)
ISBN 0-687-02625-3 (v. 6, 1–2 Kings)
ISBN 0-687-02626-1 (v. 7, 1–2 Chronicles)
ISBN 0-687-02627-X (v. 8, Ezra–Esther)
ISBN 0-687-02628-8 (v. 9, Job)
ISBN 0-687-02629-6 (v. 10, Psalms)
ISBN 0-687-02630-X (v. 11, Proverbs–Song of Solomon)
ISBN 0-687-02631-8 (v. 12, Isaiah)
ISBN 0-687-02632-6 (v. 13, Jeremiah–Lamentations)
ISBN 0-687-02633-4 (v. 14, Ezekiel–Daniel)
ISBN 0-687-02634-2 (v. 15, Hosea–Jonah)
ISBN 0-687-02635-0 (v. 16, Micah–Malachi)
ISBN 0-687-02636-9 (v. 17, Matthew)
ISBN 0-687-02637-7 (v. 18, Mark)
ISBN 0-687-02638-5 (v. 19, Luke)
ISBN 0-687-02639-3 (v. 20, John)
ISBN 0-687-02640-7 (v. 21, Acts)
ISBN 0-687-02642-3 (v. 22, Romans)
ISBN 0-687-02643-1 (v. 23, 1–2 Corinthians)
ISBN 0-687-02644-X (v. 24, Galatians–Ephesians)
ISBN 0-687-02645-8 (v. 25, Philippians–2 Thessalonians)
ISBN 0-687-02646-6 (v. 26, 1 Timothy–Philemon)
ISBN 0-687-02647-4 (v. 27, Hebrews)
ISBN 0-687-02648-2 (v. 28, James–Jude)
ISBN 0-687-02649-0 (v. 29, Revelation)
ISBN 0-687-02650-4 (complete set of 29 vols.)

94 95 96 97 98 99 00 01 02 03—10 9 8 7 6 5 4 3 2 1

MANUFACTURED IN THE UNITED STATES OF AMERICA

Contents

Outline of Samuel

1 Samuel

I. Samuel's Birth and Call (1:1–4:1*a*)
  A. Samuel's miraculous birth (1:1-28)
  B. Hannah's hymn of thanksgiving (2:1-11)
  C. Eli's wicked sons (2:12-25)
  D. Judgment against the family of Eli (2:26-36)
  E. God's revelation to Samuel (3:1–4:1*a*)
II. The Ark Narratives (4:1*b*–7:2)
  A. The Philistines' capture of the ark (4:1*b*-11)
  B. Eli's death (4:12-22)
  C. The ark's terrors among the Philistines (5:1-12)
  D. The Philistines' return of the ark (6:1–7:2)
III. Israel's Move to Monarchy (7:3–12:25)
  A. Samuel's leadership of Israel (7:3-17)
  B. Israel's demand for a king (8:1-22)
  C. Samuel's secret anointing of Saul (9:1–10:16)
  D. Saul's accession—a second account (10:17-27)
  E. Saul's rescue of Jabesh-Gilead (11:1-15)
  F. Samuel's final address (12:1-25)
IV. Saul's Rule over Israel (13:1–15:35)
  A. Escalation of the Philistine threat (13:1-7*a*)
  B. Saul's cultic offense (13:7*b*-15*a*)
  C. Israel against the Philistines (13:15*b*–14:52)
    1. Jonathan's victory at Michmash (13:15*b*–14:23)
    2. Jonathan's disobedience of Saul (14:24-46)
    3. Saul's victories (14:47-48)
    4. Saul's family (14:49-52)
  D. A second account of Saul's rejection (15:1-35)

Introduction to 1 and 2 Samuel

The Content of 1 and 2 Samuel

The books of 1 and 2 Samuel contain narratives that highlight selected events in Israelite history from the end of the period of the judges (about 1025 B.C.) until shortly before the death of King David (about 961 B.C.). The opening three chapters of 1 Samuel recount the miraculous birth of Samuel and his timely entry into the priestly service of God. Samuel quickly becomes the major transitional figure in early Israel who oversees the political move by the tribes of Israel from governance by judges to rule by kings.

Despite probable reservations, Samuel anoints Saul as Israel's first king, in response to pleas from a frightened and threatened Israel. Although Saul manages to slow the Philistine aggression on Israelite territory, he lacks the military strength to deal them the final knockout blow. Perhaps even more discouraging to Saul, God turns against him (albeit for just causes), and turns in the direction of David. Saul's jealousy and envy of David prompt the ill-fated king to plot the murder of this young and popular warrior. Understandably, this drives David into flight and hiding. As his relentless pursuit of David continues, Saul becomes increasingly unable to wage war successfully with the Philistines. Desperate for guidance, he turns to a deceased Samuel, by way of a medium, only to learn of his impending death. The very next day, the Philistines rout Samuel's army and wound the king. To avoid torture and humiliation at the hands of his enemies, Saul falls upon his own sword. First Samuel ends with an act of kindness by the men of Jabesh, when they stealthily remove the bodies of Saul and Jonathan from public display on the walls of Beth-shan and provide appropriate burials.

Second Samuel provides an account of David's reign, first over the southern tribes of Judah, then over the combined southern and northern tribes. David more than justifies his reputation as a great warrior by conquering not only the Philistines, but also the Syrians, the Amorites, the Amalekites, and many other neighboring tribes. At the height of his career, David controlled most of the territories from Syria (Aram) in the north to Elath in the south, and all the lands west and just east of the Jordan River. At no other time in her history would Israel's empire reach such broad limits!

But, for all David's accomplishments as a king and as a warrior, he seemed unable to manage his personal and domestic life with the same expertise. His adulterous affair with Bathsheba brought suffering and death to innocent persons. His mishandling of his sons, Amnon and Absalom, led to rebellion and to his temporary abdication of his royal throne in Jerusalem.

Even though David did quell Absalom's rebellion and regain his throne quickly, the latter years of his reign seethed with internal political conflicts. He faced the difficult question of succession to his throne, as well as subversive mistrust from many factions within the northern tribes. Second Samuel concludes with an act of contrition, when David erects an altar to God for having sinned in the taking of a census. This final act, however, connects the books of 1 and 2 Samuel to the book of 1 Kings, because the site of David's altar becomes the very site upon which King Solomon builds the famous Temple.

The stories of the Hebrew monarchy continue in 1 and 2 Kings, where Solomon succeeds David as king of Israel.

But the exciting stories of Samuel, Saul, and David, and the early formative days of the Israelite monarchy come to an end. The books of 1 and 2 Samuel are virtually unmatched in the Old Testament for their exciting action and for the pathos of real human experiences. Perhaps the writers of the Old Testament sensed a measure of the glory of these days when they repeatedly invested David's reign with nostalgic glory. These exciting days of early Israelite monarchy, energized by the personalities of Samuel, Saul, and David, are what 1 and 2 Samuel are all about.

The Place of 1 and 2 Samuel in the Old Testament

In the Hebrew Scriptures, 1 and 2 Samuel belong to a group of books designated as the *Former Prophets*. Included within this canonical division are the books of Joshua, Judges, 1 and 2 Samuel, and 1 and 2 Kings. These narratives provide accounts of the Israelites from their entry into Canaan (about 1240 B.C.) until their deportation at the hands of the Assyrians (722 B.C.) and the Neo-Babylonians (587 B.C.). The expression *Former Prophets* distinguishes these books from other biblical books called the *Latter Prophets:* Isaiah, Jeremiah, and Ezekiel, plus the twelve minor prophets.

That the rabbis or scribes who arranged and named these collections identified the books of Joshua, Judges, Samuel, and Kings as *Former Prophets* is interesting. It is clear that the personalities and functions of the characters in the Former Prophets are rather dissimilar to the classical Old Testament prophets such as Isaiah and Jeremiah. Saul and David are political leaders first, and spokesmen for God second. Yet, perhaps the rabbis recognized that the essential characteristic of a judge, a king, and a prophet is that special spiritual empowerment from God known as the *charismatic endowment*—that is, the Spirit of the Lord. These famous characters derive their keen insights and their outstanding leadership capacities from God's imparted strength, not from their own innate abilities. The intended chronological meaning of *former* as distinct from *latter* is unclear, but the theological continuity between the two sections clearly indicates the biblical view that God spoke to the people through a variety of persons.

Originally in early Hebrew manuscripts, 1 and 2 Samuel formed a single book on a single scroll. When the rabbis added vowels to the texts, the size of the book increased, so that a single scroll was too large to accommodate 1 and 2 Samuel as a single book. So the book was divided. About the third or second century B.C., Greek versions of the Old Testament (known as the Septuagint) combined 1 and 2 Samuel with 1 and 2 Kings, and designated the entire collection as the books of *Kingdoms*. Exactly when these scrolls were first separated into four books in Hebrew is unclear, since the Greek and Latin versions, while combining them as books of the Kingdoms, divide them onto scrolls almost exactly as 1 and 2 Samuel and 1 and 2 Kings are divided and now appear in English translations. The division of 1 and 2 Samuel following the death of Saul is appropriate for two reasons. First, these books precede the great reign of King David. Second, this division follows other Old Testament divisions. For example, the Pentateuch closes with the death of Moses rather than the more natural recapture of the Promised Land.

The name of the two books, 1 and 2 Samuel, is interesting since David is clearly the main character in one and one-half of these books. Although we cannot be certain, it seems reasonable that the writers and collectors of this material assigned it Samuel's name because he played such an important role in moving Israel from one historical period, the era of judges, to another age, the monarchy. Samuel anoints Saul king over Israel, provides council for, as well as critique of his rule, then anoints David as king when Saul sins against God. Samuel's influence on subsequent Hebrew history is considerable. And it is appropriate that the books recounting this history bear his name.

The Authorship of 1 and 2 Samuel

The authorship of 1 and 2 Samuel is complicated and controversial. The title of the books probably reflects the name of their first major character, Samuel, rather than designating actual authorship. Also, the reference in 1 Chronicles 29:29 to an unknown source, the *Chronicles of Samuel*, the *Chronicles of Nathan*, and the *Chronicles of God* probably refers to a set of documents, now lost, on which the books of Samuel and Chronicles are based, not to the Old Testament books themselves. Complicating matters further, we can hardly help noticing the duplications in these stories. (1) There are two accounts of how Saul becomes king (compare 1 Samuel 9:1–10:16 with 1 Samuel 10:17-27). (2) There are two accounts of how David enters Saul's service (compare 16:14-23 with 17:1-58). (3) There are two accounts of Saul's sin against God (compare 13:7b-15a with 15:1-35). In addition to these duplications, there are more general differences in points of view (pro-monarchy versus anti-monarchy). These factors seem to suggest that more than one writer's material has been combined into the present books of 1 and 2 Samuel. But who were these writers?

Most likely an anonymous author, or perhaps a group of authors, writing during the Babylonian Exile of the Jews (587–538 B.C.), brought together several earlier sources and wrote a history of Israel from the settlement in Canaan (13th century B.C.) until the deportation by the Neo-Babylonians (587 B.C.). The author is often referred to as the *Deuteronomistic Historian.* This historian used different sources, both written and oral, which reflected different points of view or presented different accounts of the same incident.

Two reasons may be given why an ancient writer might have used stories that present different accounts of the same event. (1) Differences in factual details were less important than the overall theological message these different accounts presented. (2) The writer may have believed that each version contained some elements of truth. Thus, to have omitted one version would have resulted in a misrepresentation of the event. In view of these considerations, we must not fault the writer for using more than one account, nor should we judge his writing in light of our own standards of coherence and consistency today.

The historian believed that the history of Israel reflected Israel's apostasy. Apostasy, the worship of other gods, was among the most serious sins a person or nation could commit. It violated the first commandment. Such sin had been forbidden in Deuteronomy 30:15-20. Israel's plight at the hands of the Assyrians and Neo-Babylonians was the direct result of her years of repeated sin. The Exile was God's punishment of the Israelites. To document the justice of God's punishment, the writer retells the history of Israel, clearly showing how king after king allowed the people to fall victim to apostasy. The often-used phrase, *They did what was evil in the sight of the LORD*, usually refers to the king's apostasy.

Among the sources used by the historian are the following: (1) the ark narratives (1 Samuel 4–7; 2 Samuel 6; 7), (2) the Saul stories (1 Samuel 9:1–10:16; 11; 13–14), (3) the court history of David (2 Samuel 9; 1 Kings 2). In addition to these three larger, more clearly recognizable blocks of material, the writer used stories about Samuel's childhood (1 Samuel 1–3), David's early days (1 Samuel 16), and various hymns and lists. The writer arranged these sources, added his own comments, and superimposed an interpretative perspective to reflect his own theological point of view. As the commentary unfolds, these particular sources will be discussed further, with explanations about how the writer shaped the material to reflect his particular point of view.

Israel's History During These Years

Although the precise details of Israel's history during the years of Samuel, Saul, and David are difficult for us to reconstruct today, the Bible does supply us with a reliable outline of the sequence of events. As indicated above, these books bear the unmistakable imprint of the historian's work. His concern to provide a theological interpretation of history limited his discussions of the economic, political, and cultural aspects of monarchical history. Even so, most scholars feel that these biblical accounts can help us reconstruct an accurate history of this early period.

As we move into the later reigns of David and Solomon, our history becomes even more detailed due to more reliable sources. Also, we can now make use of archaeological investigations of sites such as Shiloh, Megiddo, Gilbeah, Arad, Hazor, and Gezer.

The chronological limits for the period described in 1 and 2 Samuel extend from approximately 1030–1025 B.C. (Samuel, Saul) until 961 B.C. (David's death). During this fifty- to sixty-year period, the political organization of Israel changed from a loosely assembled group of semi-nomadic tribes and small Canaanite city-states to a relatively large urban state with all of the distinguishing features, such as a common religion, a standing army, a capital city, and cumbersome governmental bureaucracy.

As David's empire stabilized, manufacturing and international trade began to emerge. The young nation, Israel, flexed its territorial muscles with no Egyptians and no Assyrians to limit its appetite. Under David's leadership, Israel extended its sphere of influence from the Euphrates River in the north to Elath in the south at the Gulf of Aqaba, and from the Transjordan to the Mediterranean Sea. Israel had truly come of age! But how did Israel get to this point in history? What roles did Samuel and Saul play in the formation of this new state?

During the last quarter of the eleventh century, when Samuel came into prominence as a judge, the word *Israel* referred to a loosely organized group of tribes living in Canaan and in the Transjordan. These tribes functioned independently, except perhaps during times of severe political crisis.

Several leading Old Testament scholars believe that some of these tribes periodically assembled to worship God and to celebrate a common historical heritage (Deuteronomy 26:5 and following). Although there may well have been other sanctuaries these tribes used, the sites of Shiloh and Shechem are mentioned most often as the locations of fall and spring festivals. This common religion could have served as an initial source of unity and attraction during times of peace. What does seem clear is that originally semi-nomadic tribes infiltrated Canaan and gradually became dominant politically, at least in certain regions in the central hill country and in the valleys to the north. Yet they were not the only intruders into Palestine.

Following their expulsion from Egypt around 1200 B.C., the Philistines relocated in the sparsely settled coastal regions in southwestern Canaan (Gaza, Ashdod, Ekron). Over the next half-century, these highly skilled warriors needed and desired additional territory, then occupied by Canaanites and by the tribes of Israel. Their strong centralized government more naturally lent itself to military aggressiveness than did the loose tribal confederacy system among the Israelites.

Soon after their occupation, the Philistines gained control of the iron industry in Palestine and forced the Israelites into dependency for the purchase of manufactured wares as well as the service on these wares (1 Samuel 13:19-21). Archaic Israelite weaponry was no match for Philistine chariots, spears, and daggers of iron. With increasing frequency the Philistines pushed northward toward the fertile valleys of Esdraelon and the occupied hill country in central Canaan. Meanwhile, Israel also began to expand beyond earlier occupied territories. An inevitable collision ensued in the central hill country, resulting in numerous battles between the tribes of Israel and the Philistines.

A principal battle in the conflict occurred at Aphek, resulting in a decisive victory for the Philistines and a devastating loss for Israel. Since the Philistines seemed to have possessed superior military skills, as well as controlling the available iron supply, they indeed posed a serious threat to the continued survival of Israel. Even worse, the defeat at Aphek not only cost Israel valuable territory, but the Philistines also captured the famous ark.

To provide more effective centralized leadership, Samuel anointed Saul of Gibeah as king. Unlike his predecessors (the judges), Saul did not disband his army once the Philistine threat was temporarily checked, but instead retained it, and monarchy became a permanent institution. Saul's relatively brief reign was characterized by almost constant warfare with one hostile tribe or another. He was also plagued with internal dissension, recalcitrant tribes (Gibeonites), and by his uncontrollable jealousy of David. As if these military and psychological problems were not a sufficient depressant, Saul also had to cope with the loss of support from Samuel, climaxing in a fateful severance between the two men, with God in full support of Samuel.

The length of Saul's reign is unclear (1 Samuel 13:1), as is the extent of his new kingdom. Most of his power was centered in the northern territories of Benjamin, Ephraim, and Gilead. Yet he apparently had considerable support in both Galilee and Judah. Saul's reign ended with his disastrous defeat by the Philistines and his death by his own hand. Since so much of the Saul material is shaped by pro-Davidic writers, this very able ruler probably receives less credit than he actually deserves.

David's reign propelled Israel to her greatest heights of national and international prominence. The tribes in the loose arrangement of the older confederacy quickly attached themselves to this young, vigorous leader who offered safety and security. Within a very few years after becoming king of Judah at Hebron, David accepted a mandate to rule all Israel. He lost no time in conquering the Philistines completely, and then he restricted their territory to the southwest portions of his country. The Philistine menace to Israel was ended permanently.

Next, David moved quickly to bring additional territories under his control, including Syria, Edom, Moab, Amnon, and others. The previously unconquered Jebusite city of Jerusalem was conquered and named capital of a united country, Israel. David's once small mercenary army had, by this time, swollen to considerable size, with volunteers from many other tribes and segments of society. Israel was now a nation like other nations, in virtually every sense of the word.

But Israelite monarchy was not without its critics, and many of the tribes that had come to David in times of military emergency longed for their independence in times of peace. Also, prophetic voices warned of the potential danger of idolatry inherent within the institution of kingship itself. Even within the royal palace greed, jealousy, and political intrigue darkened the glory of David's reign. Personal weakness of King David heightened his internal discord. But due to excellent support from his loyal subjects, as well as misdeeds of others, David managed to retain his throne and calm his critics.

Yet, the latter days of David's reign were still filled with bitter intrigue and subversion in the matter of succession. Which of David's remaining sons was to follow him as king? The outcome of this palace soap opera must remain unresolved until 1 Kings.

David left a legacy in Israelite history that is yet to be equaled. While it may be true that international politics certainly favored David's territorial expansion, David will always stand out as the central figure in Israelite monarchy. In Jerusalem even today the tomb of David stands in honor of Israel's greatest king.

Major Theological Themes in 1 and 2 Samuel

The material in 1 and 2 Samuel has been shaped and edited according to the theological beliefs of the historian. Theological intentions outweigh factual accuracy in his portrayal of the history of Israel. Yet he is a true historian in the very best sense of that term. He is an interpreter of events occurring in day-to-day affairs. From the writer's point of view, Israel's entire history, from settlement to exile, is replete with apostasy.

Using Deuteronomy 30:15-20 as his theological norm, the writer documents repeated instances where Israel worshiped other gods. He focuses on apostasy to the extent of ignoring other historical factors such as economic and political circumstances. Other than David, Hezekiah, and Josiah, few of Israel's and Judah's rulers upheld the first commandment: *You shall have no other gods before me* (Exodus 20:3). God's punishment for their sins should have come as no surprise to Israel, for prophet after prophet announced the approaching judgment of God (Isaiah 2:6-22; Amos 2:4-5, 6-7).

And upon whom should blame be placed for the catastrophe of 587 B.C.? The writer clearly places responsibility on the shoulders of the rulers. Israel's and Judah's kings committed evil in the sight of the Lord. And as the kings worshiped foreign gods, so did the general population. As the Lord of history, God will not long tolerate repeated violations of the commandments. Even powerful nations such as Babylon and Assyria move to the Lord's beat.

This panoramic view of Israel's place within world history clearly acknowledged the writer's faith in God as the ruler of history. And the particular history of Israel constituted a graphic, if tragic, witness to God's powerful arm. Just as many an individual discovers that personal sin does not long go unpunished, so too does Israel experience God's judgment resulting from this collective sin. For the writer, the final word in Israel's history was not national political strength or weakness, economic prosperity or poverty, or any other conventional standard. For him, Israel's history, as measured by obedience to God's word, was clearly sinful. And this disobedience intensified during the monarchy.

A second set of theological themes in 1 and 2 Samuel focuses on different forms of divine revelation. The writer interpreted Israel's history as displaying God's awesome presence, both for deliverance as well as for judgment. But in addition to this more general revelation for the nation, particular individuals also received God's word: Samuel (1 Samuel 3:1–4:1*a*), Nathan (2 Samuel 7:4-16), and David. Through disclosures to these special persons, God's will was revealed to Israel and Judah.

Yet a third form in which Israel discerned God's presence was in the famous ark of the covenant, first attended by Eli at Shiloh, then later by David in Jerusalem. Certainly for the tribes of the north, the ark represented the dynamic presence of God. The Philistines who captured this holy relic quickly learned of its power. The havoc it wrought in the cities of Ashdod and Ekron attested to God's anger.

A fourth form of personal revelation appearing in 1 and 2 Samuel is God's special form of empowering a leader through the charismatic endowment—the indwelling of God's spirit. Samuel, and the judges who ruled before him, received this power, and delivered Israel out of the hands of its aggressors. Initially Saul experienced God's imparted strength in a powerful way, and successfully rescued Jabesh. But his later disobedience angered the Lord, who retracted the gift and gave it to David instead.

God's covenant with David provides yet another theological theme of great importance in 1 and 2 Samuel. In 2 Samuel 7, Nathan tells David that the Lord does not desire a house (temple), but instead will build David a "house." In return for David's loyal and devoted service, God agrees to establish David as one of the world's great rulers, whose fame reached foreign capitals; to provide David and his country peace and security; and to perpetuate the Davidic dynasty forever.

The Davidic covenant provided a theological justification for monarchy and quieted objections from conservative elements in the north. Kingship was now a legitimate institution. David was elevated to a theological stature comparable to figures such as Abraham and Moses.

A fifth theological theme in these two books is the nature of servanthood. What does it mean to be a true servant of the Lord? Judging from the stories and characters in 1 and 2 Samuel, three traits are essential: (1) obedience to God's word, (2) a sense of morality (even if imperfect in execution), and (3) a loyalty to God. Samuel and David both exhibited these qualities, as did many other Old Testament figures. Human perfection (freedom from sin) is not a prerequisite for servanthood, but consciousness of God's expectation does clearly distinguish God's person.

Finally, we should add a word on the nature of early Hebrew conception of afterlife—Sheol. As is clear from 1 Samuel 28:3-25, deceased persons all go to Sheol, a dark, dismal place somewhere below the surface of the earth where one engages in little or no activity, nor desires to do so. A doctrine of heaven as a future reward for the faithful is not yet a tenet of religious faith. Divine retribution plays no role in a person's post-death sojourn. But it is clear that death, even at this stage of Hebrew thought, is not a terminal experience. All persons end up in Sheol.

1 Samuel 1–3

Introduction to These Chapters

The opening three chapters in 1 Samuel present accounts of three closely related incidents: (1) the miraculous and timely birth of Samuel, (2) the moral decadence of the house of Eli, priest at Shiloh, and (3) the prophetic call of Samuel, elevating him into God's service. Originally, these stories arose and circulated independently. But the writer has carefully blended them together, forming a continuous and coherent narrative.

Here is an outline of 1 Samuel 1–3.
 I. Samuel's Miraculous Birth (1:1-28)
 II. Hannah's Hymn of Thanksgiving (2:1-11)
 III. Eli's Wicked Sons (2:12-25)
 IV. Judgment Against the Family of Eli (2:26-36)
 V. God's Revelation to Samuel (3:1–4:1a)

Samuel's Miraculous Birth (1:1-28)

These verses identify Samuel's home and his family lineage. Ramathaim is a village located in Ephraim, a region in the hill country of central Israel. However, later in verse 19, Samuel's home is identified as Ramah, a village located (probably) in Benjaminite territory. The Hebrew word *ramah* means *height* or *high place,* and could refer to any one of several different locations, some of which are located in Benjamin, while others are in Ephraim. It is therefore uncertain from these references whether Samuel's home is located in Ephraim or in Benjamin. Perhaps, however, the identification of

Samuel's relative Zuph (area of *Zuph*, 1 Samuel 9:5), also referred to as an Ephraimite (verse 1), tips the scales in favor of Ramathaim in Ephraim as Samuel's home. Shiloh is the early Israelite cultic center, located approximately twenty miles northeast of Jerusalem. Shiloh is the dwelling place of the famous ark of the covenant, the central religious object of the early Israelite tribes. Samuel serves as an apprentice priest at Shiloh, and it is here that he spends most of his youth.

Samuel's father is Elkanah, a man of important lineage and great piety. The specific persons to whom he is related are unknown to us, as they are mentioned only in a parallel story in 1 Chronicles 6:26-27. In the Chronicles text, Samuel is associated with a Levitical ancestry.

Samuel's mother, Hannah, is mentioned first among Elkanah's wives, suggesting possibly that she is preferred by her husband. Unfortunately, Hannah has borne her husband no children. This barren condition, as well as Elkanah's obvious favoritism, brings derision from Peninnah, Elkanah's other wife. Having more than one wife was a common feature of ancient Israelite society, primarily for two reasons: (1) to ensure a sufficient number of male heirs, and (2) to provide a home for otherwise destitute and dependent women.

Childlessness was often perceived as a sign of divine punishment, but here, as with Rebekah (Genesis 25:21), it provides opportunity for God's intervention. There is no evidence that Hannah has offended God.

Elkanah's great piety is shown by his annual pilgrimages to Shiloh, where he worships God at a seasonal harvest celebration. This act of worship is a family affair, involving both Elkanah and his wives.

The physical nature of the sanctuary at Shiloh is difficult to determine. We do not know if this site contained a tent housing the ark, or was a permanent structure. However, we do know that Shiloh was a very important site in early Israelite religion (see 1 Kings

14:1-2). In Jeremiah 7:12, Shiloh is identified as having been destroyed as the object of God's wrathful judgment. The phrase LORD of hosts in verse 3 (NRSV; NIV, LORD Almighty) is the full name of Israel's God. It refers to God's leadership, both of the army during holy war, and more generally of the nation through the religious cult and the ark. For the moment at least, the Lord of hosts resides at Shiloh, and moves about by way of the ark of the covenant. Hannah's vow (verse 11) to leave her future son's head unshaven reflects a practice of an ancient cult known as the Nazirites. This cult was well-known in early Israel for its piety and absolute devotion to God.

The priestly staff at Shiloh is introduced briefly in verse 3—Eli and his sons Hophni and Phinehas. No credentials distinguish them. The fact that they serve at Shiloh indicates their high standing in the cultic community. At this point in the story, no hint is given the reader that ominous days loom large on the horizon for this family. Not even Eli's mistaken assumption about Hannah's mumbling detracts from his character or credentials. His blessing upon her and his reassurance of God's aid are both fitting and laudable acts for a priest.

God answers Hannah's prayer and she gives birth to a son. In turn, she keeps her vow. After a proper period of time, she returns to Shiloh and enters Samuel into the priestly service of God, under Eli's tutelage.

Hannah's Hymn of Thanksgiving (2:1-11)

In terms of style and theme, this elegant poetic composition may be classified as a hymn of thanksgiving. It is similar in structure to other such psalms in the Old Testament (Psalms 107; 136; 138; Jonah 2:2-9). Thematically, it celebrates God's miraculous gift of a son to a childless woman. As is often true in the Old Testament, God elevates lowly persons to pinnacles of great height. The weak become mighty, not of their own accord, but solely because of God's strengthening grace. Overwhelmed by gratitude, Hannah's only appropriate response is to burst forth rejoicing with a song of thanksgiving. Mary, the mother of Jesus, sings a similar song in the New Testament (Luke 1:46-55).

The expression *my strength* (NRSV) literally means *my horn* (NIV). The image is a horned animal proudly tossing its head to and fro as a symbol of strength. God has distinguished this woman, Hannah, in a visible way. Her lowly, barren situation has been transformed into ecstatic delight.

The term *holy* refers to the *otherness* of God. *Rock* is a standard symbol of power and might (see Isaiah 44:8).

The theme of God empowering the powerless stands at the center of this great hymn. God elevates the weak, the helpless, and the lowly. To such persons God brings honor and glory.

The phrase *pillars of the earth* (verse 8; NRSV; NIV, *foundations of the earth*) reflects an ancient Near Eastern view that envisions the earth as a flat disk, supported by pillars. Below the earth is Sheol and above lies heaven, God's home. Sheol is the dwelling place of the dead.

Verse 9-10 reaffirm God's justice in the world. God rewards faithful servants, but brings punishment to all those persons who disobey.

The phrase *strength to his king* is clearly anachronistic. It places the actual composition of this hymn at a time further along during the monarchy, since, as yet, Israel has no king. Yet, the reference in verse 5*b* to the barren woman who gave birth to children clearly relates the theme of this great song to Hannah's situation. As matters stand in the biblical account of Israel's history, Hannah's hymn of thanksgiving is an appropriate and uplifting response to her moment of joy.

The term *anointed* refers to the king whom the Lord blesses. In Hebrew, the word is *messiah*. In special ceremonies, Israelite kings were anointed by God's duly appointed representatives, the priests, and thereby received their power to rule effectively.

Eli's Wicked Sons (2:12-25)

Three principal points emerge in these verses: (1) the reprehensible conduct of Hophni and Phinehas, Eli's sons; (2) the meteoric rise of Samuel as God's special servant; and (3) the ominous announcement of the downfall of the Elide priesthood. Clearly, these diverse events are closely related. Precisely because of the cultiç and moral infractions committed by Hophni and Phinehas, God intends to replace Eli and his family with a more faithful priest. As the abuses at the Shiloh sanctuary continue to mount, angering God even more, Samuel distinguishes himself more and more with God and Israel. Finally, in a climactic narrative in chapter 3, Samuel is called into the full confidence of God and becomes the pre-eminent spokesman for the Lord in Israel. With certainty and clarity, God manages the affairs of the world through the lives of chosen servants, indeed even through evil ones.

The phrase *had no regard for the* LORD (verse 12) refers to Hophni and Phinehas and their cultic sins. These irreverent men lack proper respect for God, and for the things of God. Their disregard for traditional sacrificial practice ignites the fire of God's wrath. And God's anger does not go unexpressed (verses 27-36) for long.

Evidently, the procedure for offering a sacrifice to God at Shiloh entailed certain specified activities. Following the slaughter of the sacrificial animal and the proper handling of its blood on the altar, the fatty portions were separated and then burned as an offering. Next, the lean meat remaining was boiled. The service concluded with a ceremonial meal, where the worshipers consumed the remaining meat. Since the priest who presided over the sacrifice was due compensation, he received what he could remove by thrusting a special three-pronged spear into the boiling pot of lean meat. But he was not allowed to select raw meat before it had been ceremonially offered to God. This procedure insured that God received proper honor by receiving the choicest and purest portions—even before the priest.

Here, however, Hophni and Phinehas violate protocol and thus profane God's offering by selecting portions from the raw meat before the fat has been ceremonially proffered to God. They also take the lean meat before it has been boiled. This sacrilege offends God. These sins are unpardonable; no atonement can be made for them.

Compounding these cultic violations further, Hophni and Phinehas sin once more by forcing sexual favors from women attending the Shiloh sanctuary. There is no indication here that these women are to be considered cultic prostitutes, as in Baal religion. Instead, the women probably perform various tasks necessary to the maintenance of God's shrine. Their positions are thus honorable and necessary, making the improper advances of Eli's sons even more of a moral outrage. And even though Eli admonishes them repeatedly to cease at once, they refuse to listen. God has hardened their hearts. God has sealed their fate because of their earlier cultic violations.

Meanwhile, Samuel is increasing in God's favor. The linen ephod is a type of apron or waist-cloak signifying his priestly office. This little garment is, as is some of his upkeep, supplied by his family. Elkhanah and Hannah continue to receive blessings at God's hand, for they have loaned God this little priest.

Judgment Against the Family of Eli (2:22-36)

An anonymous *man of God* boldly heralds God's judgment against Eli and his family. They are to be replaced by a more faithful priest—probably Zadok (1 Kings 2:27)—in time. But for the moment, Samuel seems the intended object of God's pleasure. Certainly God's decision to punish the corrupt priests at Shiloh spells disaster for Eli, Hophni, and Phinehas.

The mention of *your fathers* (NIV; NRSV, *your ancestor*) in verse 27 refers to Aaron and his priestly descendants. There seems to be a rather clear lineage linking Aaron with Eli and Abiathar. The latter is eventually replaced as priest by Zadok, once Solomon takes the throne following David's death.

God's Revelation to Samuel (3:1–4:1*a*)

This chapter is the climax of the Samuel narrative up to this point. God's words to Samuel, a priest, now establish him as a prophet, a legitimate spokesman for the Lord to all Israel. With this calling, and the insights it brings, Samuel matures into the religious and political leader of Israel. We now begin to realize that this truly remarkable person was no mere accident of history. Even before his birth, Samuel was destined for leadership of God's people. And now he is ready to begin this task.

But Chapter 3 also reconfirms God's decision to punish Eli and his sons. As difficult as it must have been for Samuel to convey such a gloomy message to his priestly mentor, he accepts this responsibility. The announcement of judgment by the anonymous prophet in 2:31 is reconfirmed. The Elide priesthood now begins its demise with the deaths of Hophni and Phinehas, leading up to the banishment of Abiathar by King Solomon (1 Kings 2:27).

The *word of the* LORD in verse 1 refers to God's revelation. It is a formal expression used frequently by the classical Old Testament prophets to refer their announcements of judgment to God. Evidently, because of the atrocities at the Shiloh sanctuary, God had chosen to withdraw from Israel. God had become conspicuously silent. God's revelation to Samuel is even more unusual and timely, given the dearth of God's word at this time.

The *lamp of God* refers to a sacred object placed inside the sanctuary, close to the ark, as prescribed by Mosaic law (Exodus 25:31-40). This lamp is to burn all night to symbolize the abiding presence of God. Thus the phrase *had not yet gone out* suggests that it is almost dawn. Exactly why Samuel is sleeping beside the ark is unclear.

The ark of God was the primary religious object of early Israel. It was a chest, conveyed by two poles that did not actually touch the sacred object itself. Much more will be said about the ark in the next section, since it occupies a prominent role in chapters 4–6.

Verse 7 states that *Samuel did not yet know the* LORD. He has not experienced firsthand God's holy presence. God is real to him, but not personal or intimate.

May God do so to you and more also (3:17 NRSV; NIV, *May God deal with you, be it ever so severely*) is a customary oath in the Old Testament. It involves God in the particular situation, thereby guaranteeing the truth and trustworthiness of the desired testimony. Eli's stoic response to Samuel's disclosure reveals a man whose faith in God extends even into the acceptance of judgment.

The phrase *let none of his words fall to the ground* means that God's words, as delivered by Samuel, are true words. They actually come to pass—events happen as they are announced. *From Dan to Beersheba* designates the territorial limits, north to south, of all Israel.

§ § § § § § §

The Message of 1 Samuel 1–3

These opening chapters of 1 Samuel raise several important theological issues. These issues are embedded in the narratives in such a way that they reflect particular theological convictions; they are not included as doctrine. In early Israel theology was primarily an activity, not a set of dogmatic propositions.

The issues raised include (1) the close connection between religion and politics; (2) the mysterious nature of divine revelation; (3) the nature of sin; (4) divine determinism; (5) God's special help for the helpless; and (6) divine retribution.

§ § § § § § §

1 Samuel 4–6

Introduction to These Chapters

With no transition the historian leaves the stories about Samuel's emerging leadership of Israel and jumps to several humorous episodes featuring the famous ark. Such an abrupt break in consecutive narratives suggests that the historian has shifted to a source different from the one he followed in chapters 1–3.

Yet there is some continuity between 1:3 and 4:6, with the capture of the ark and its portentous departure from Shiloh. Perhaps this removal of God's presence prepares the way for God's termination of the Elide priesthood and its former leadership of Israel at Shiloh.

Hophni and Phinehas die quickly and with little attention or comment. And Eli suffers a fatal fall upon learning that the ark has been captured. As for Shiloh, it seems to vanish as the central cultic site among the northern tribes, only to be mentioned later by prophets as having been the object of God's punishment.

These three chapters describe the serious threat the Philistines pose to Israelite sovereignty over the land. Israel will have no easy time dispelling these aggressors from Hebrew territory.

Here is an outline of chapters 4–6.
  I. The Philistines' Capture of the Ark (4:1b-11)
  II. Eli's Death (4:12-22)
  III. The Ark's Terrors Among the Philistines (5:1-12)
  IV. The Philistines' Return of the Ark (6:1–7:2)

The Philistines' Capture of the Ark (4:1b-11)

Toward the end of the thirteenth century or at the beginning of the twelfth century B.C., the entire Mediterranean costal region from Egypt to Syria experienced a tremendous upheaval as a result of invaders known from Egyptian records as the Sea People. They first attempted to enter Egypt, but were quickly repelled. They then moved northward and settled along the coastal plain of Canaan. These tribes, along with their descendants, became known as the Philistines. Although their influence was brief, at least in the larger history of the region, it was sufficiently important to furnish the land with its common name, Palestine. Their holdings originally included the regions bracketed by the cities of Gaza, Ashkelon, Ashdad, Ekron, and Gath. Some scholars believe these groups came originally from Caphtor (Crete) (Amos (9:7; Jeremiah 47:4-5). Their centralized governmental system lent itself well to aggressive military programs, and they were not long in initiating attacks upon regions then occupied by the Israelite tribes. Saul spent most of his reign doing battle with the Philistines. Not until David were they silenced permanently. But meanwhile, they posed a serious threat to cities and regions held by Israel.

The exact location of Ebenezer is unknown. Obviously, it is relatively close to Aphek, which lies only a few miles from modern Tel Aviv. The importance of this general region was considerable for both military as well as commercial reasons. These two important sites, along with Megiddo and the Esdraelon Valley, stood as crucial junctions as troops or caravans moved from the Levant to Africa. Also, Ebenezer and Aphek afforded the Philistines additional sites for expansion to accommodate their agricultural and population needs.

The high numbers of soldiers mentioned here (verse 2) and in verse 10 are probably exaggerations. Often in the

Old Testament numbers have special significance, but here they simply indicate a substantial contingent of troops. Warfare between the Israelites and the Philistines at this point in time definitely favored the latter. The Philistines probably had vastly superior weaponry, including armaments of iron and chariots. Also, their military organization seemed to provide more tactical advantage than loose assemblage of tribal representation from Israel. They exhibited this superiority by rapidly advancing into the central hill country. Their chariots gave them greater mobility and speed, especially in the open plains. The small, ill-equipped, untrained volunteer armies from the Israelite tribes were a poor match, indeed, for the Palestines. The old systems for the conduct of warfare used by Israel soon collapsed under the weight of Philistine assault.

The ark of the covenant was a portable chest, long an essential part of the religious cult of early Israel. Originally, this box contained the two tablets on which the Ten Commandments were inscribed, along with other important reminders of Israel's special relationship with God. At some point, further ornamentation was added in the form of angelic figures, the cherubim, forming a throne or seat of God. Thus, as the Israelites entered Canaan, they transported God by means of the ark. God's awesome presence virtually assured them of victory. It is little wonder, then, that when word reached their troops that the ark had been brought into the Israelite camp, the Philistines trembled in fear.

The term *Hebrew* was generally used by a foreigner to disparage the tribes of Israel. It was an expression of disdain and contempt.

Eli's Death (4:12-22)

The reactions to the disastrous events of the Aphek battle are told with considerable pathos and care. The aged but ever-vigilant priest topples to his death from atop the city gate, where he has been anxiously awaiting news of the battle. His daughter-in-law is likewise utterly distraught. She goes into premature labor and dies, just after giving birth to a child, Ichabod. These two reactions symbolize the pitiable plight of all the Israelites when they learn the ark has fallen into enemy hands. It is a sad day for Israel and for the house of Eli. Not even the birth of little Ichabod can bring cheer to a despondent and troubled nation. God has left the people.

The distance from Aphek to Shiloh is approximately twenty miles, over hilly terrain. The Benjaminite runner performs quite a remarkable feat. His appearance, with torn garments and earth heaped upon his head, are traditional symbols of mourning. Apart from connecting the runner, or perhaps the event itself, to Saul, who is from this tribe, the identification of the anonymous runner as a Benjaminite is odd.

Note that Eli does not react to the news of his son's death or of the defeat of Israel. The important news is the loss of the sacred ark. The reference to Eli's having judged Israel for forty years (verse 18*b*) is unusual, since nowhere else in the Old Testament is he identified as a judge. This term refers to the early political leaders of the tribes, such as Samson and Gideon. Eli is a priest.

The custom of calling newborn children by symbolic names is common in the Old Testament. (See Isaiah 8;1-4; Hosea 1:4-8.) Here, Israel's present plight is expressed through the name of the child, Ichabod (*the glory is gone*). The sacred ark has been captured by an enemy, leaving Israel without a clear and visible divine presence. This narrative expresses the full pathos and sorrow of the hour. Death hangs over Shiloh like a cloak. God's illuminating presence has been eclipsed by the loss of the ark.

The Ark's Terrors Among the Philistines (5:1-12)

With chapter 5, the biblical writer turns from the gloomy scene at Shiloh to the premature victory celebration of the Philistines. With the captured ark in tow, the Philistines return to Ashdod and proudly display the prized object in a submissive posture inside the temple of Dagon, their god. But this elation is short-lived, for matters are not really as they seem. God is about to turn Israel's defeat into victory.

When the Philistines capture the ark of the covenant, they achieve the pinnacle of success of one nation over another nation. Imprisoning an enemy's deity symbolizes ultimate victory—equal to the taking of prisoners of war or even the king. This is the absolute proof of supremacy. The Philistines return to Ashdod and display the Israelite spoils for all to see. The ark is put into their temple, alongside Dagon, the Philistine god. But subsequent events soon make this victory less than satisfying.

The city of Ashdod was located a few miles inland from the coast and almost in the center of Philistine territory. Five cities, each with political autonomy, constituted the heart of Philistine occupation. The cities were Ashdod, Gaza, Ekron, Ashkelon, and Gath.

Dagon was the chief god of the Philistines. This deity was known and worshiped throughout Syria and Canaan during most of the Bronze Age (3000–1200 B.C.). From the etymology of his name (clouds, rain), Dagon must have been a fertility god. When the Philistines entered Canaan, Dagon was probably already being worshiped by the native inhabitants. The newcomers simply adopted the god of the land they conquered.

Verse 5 belongs to a literary genre known as *etiology*. This genre refers to stories told to explain ancient customs, unusual geological formations, or even ethnic groups. Here we are told of the origin of a cultic practice whereby priests avoiding stepping on the threshold at the temple entrance.

The Hebrew text of 1 Samuel 5 is filled with textual problems. There are variations among the different translations from Hebrew to Greek to Latin to English. In

5:6, the Greek translation (Septuagint) adds a phrase telling of an invasion of rats carrying a plague baccillus. This phrase is probably a correct addition to the Hebrew text, in the light of 6:5. Textual problems notwithstanding, the basic plot of this humorous incident is clear. The joy and exhilaration following the Philistine capture of the Israelite ark turn into death and disaster. What initially seems to be a day of jubilation turns into a day of absolute devastation. In its present context, this brief episode serves two very important purposes. (1) It provides opportunity for God to punish the Elide priest, and thereby end the role of Shiloh as the central sanctuary for the northern tribes. (2) It provides God an occasion to punish the enemies of Israel.

The Philistines' Return of the Ark (6:1–7:2)

Chapter 6 completes this cycle of ark stories, and concludes with the return of the sacred chest to Israelite soil. With pestilence and death ravaging their cities, the Philistine leaders meet to decide how to rid themselves of these calamities. Correctly, they identify the cause to be the ark. They devise a plan to return this captured relic, appease an angry God, and thereby restore health to their territory. When the Israelites at Beth-shemesh see the ark returning aboard a cow-pulled cart, they rejoice and call for a great sacrificial celebration. For reasons not altogether clear, God becomes enraged at some of the participants and decides to punish them. Finally the ark is delivered to Kiriath-jearim where it is attended by a certain Eleazar. Chaos has abated among the Philistines, and the ark of God once again rests among the Israelites.

With great turmoil rampaging through Philistine villages, the leaders meet to devise a plan to end this situation as quickly as possible. *Seven months* is a very long time, and God's reprisal has not gone unrecognized. The *priests* and *diviners* are professional personnel who are skilled in religious affairs. Their presence is necessary to determine how best to rid the territory of the ark.

The nature of the guilt offering accompanying the ark is twofold: (1) It serves as appeasement to an angry God, and (2) it offers a product of value to an offended people. Perhaps also the visual representation of the tumors and mice suggests elements of magic. Clearly, the Philistines are sparing no expense to resolve their unfortunate plight. *Hardening of the heart* indicates Philistine familiarity with the Exodus experience. In 4:8, the details recalling the mighty acts of God are inaccurate, either to show Philistine ignorance or as a joke. But here the allusion points to the futility of resisting Israel's powerful God.

The unyoked cow and the newly constructed cart (verse 7) meet requirements for purity. Again, the offering appeasing God must be effective, for the Philistine tolerance of God's wrath has worn thin. Everything must be perfect! Also, an unyoked ox would be an untrained animal, so it would be unfamiliar with the path home. Its return to Israelite territory would clearly be the result of divine leadership, confirming suspicions that the plagues and boils were brought about by God and were not accidental.

Verses 17-18 are an etiology for a certain geological formation. A great stone serves as an altar on which to offer sacrifice, celebrating the return of the ark.

In verses 19-20, the reason for God's punitive anger is unclear. Perhaps the victims (numbers are exaggerated) lack proper jubilation over the return of the ark. Or possibly there are no priests to manage the ark. At any rate, God's anger breaks out with disastrous consequences, and a considerable number of persons die. God's ark is not common and must be treated with respect. The Philistines learn well that God's power can turn affairs upside down. But now that the ark is back in Israelite hands, they hope matters will return to normal.

§ § § § § § §

The Message of 1 Samuel 4–6

The theme of these chapters is God's awesome power.
When the Philistines captured the ark, they thought they
had captured a valuable prize. But God almost
immediately turned their celebration into mourning. God
humiliated Dagon (their god), sent a pestilence of rats,
and caused an outbreak of plague. God's power
completely overwhelmed the stunned Philistines. While
they had heard of God's earlier destruction of Pharaoh's
armies, they had no notion of the terrible chaos God
could cause. They learned very quickly what it meant to
offend God.

But the Philistines are not the only ones in these
chapters to feel the sting of God's whip. When the men of
Beth-shemesh were careless with the newly returned ark,
God lashed out at them, and many of their number were
killed. Even God's own people cowered in awe of this
mighty God, Yahweh.

Yahweh's awesome power is a theme repeated and
illustrated countless times in the Old Testament. God
unleashed the plagues upon Egypt, brought down the
mighty walls of Jericho, and caused the sun to stand still.
But even further, God created the world and all that is
therein! And after realizing that human sin was here to
stay, God began devising powerful and effective ways of
redemption. The entire Bible, from Genesis to Revelation,
witnesses to God's awesome power that can be
destructive as well as redemptive.

§ § § § § § §

1 Samuel 7–12

Introduction to These Chapters

Almost as abruptly as the narrator switched to the ark narrative in 3:21, he shifts back to the Samuel stories at 7:3 and continues his account of Samuel's leadership in Israel. Chronologically, several years have lapsed between events in 3:21 and 7:3. Samuel is now an adult and is the undisputed religious and political leader of all Israel. He functions both as a judge (7:15) and as a seer (9:1–10:16), roles that reflect different sources or traditions.

With these chapters, the writer begins to intertwine two different accounts of the origin of monarchy. Some scholars refer to these as the pro-monarchy account and the anti-monarchy account, reflective of their attitude toward kingship. In the commentary section, these stands of tradition will be identified where appropriate.

Here is an outline of these chapters.

  I. Samuel's Leadership of Israel (7:3-17)
 II. Israel's Demand for a King (8:1-22)
III. Samuel's Secret Anointing of Saul (9:1–10:16)
 IV. Saul's Accession—A Second Account (10:17-27)
  V. Saul's Rescue of Jabesh-gilead (11:1-15)
 VI. Samuel's Final Address (12:1-25)

Samuel's Leadership of Israel (7:3-17)

First Samuel 7:3-4 announces Samuel's warnings against Israelite affection for the Canaanite cults of Baal.

The writer considers apostasy the paramount sin. The name *Baal* applies to several male deities worshiped in Canaanite religion. In fact, the Baals are represented in many forms in Canaanite theology and are worshiped at numerous cultic centers throughout the country. Baal's female consorts are known as *Ashtaroth.*

Together, these male and female fertility deities are believed to exercise significant influence over the agricultural life of that country. As the Israelites become increasingly sedentary, Canaanite agricultural practices seem attractive, and superior to the more pastoral pursuits of semi-nomads. Naturally, the gods who are worshiped by the Canaanite farmers seem better able to help than Israel's God. Accordingly, apostasy poses a major temptation to the religious beliefs of early Israelites. Samuel reminds them of the dangers resulting from apostasy (Judges 2:11-15).

The second section of this chapter describes God's miraculous defeat of the Philistines, further vindicating Samuel's capable leadership of Israel. In a scene that reminds us of several similar situations described in the book of Judges, Israel is ablaze with fear of the Philistines. The people plead with Samuel to lead them in a cultic act of purification, which he willingly performs. God responds to this expression of faith by routing the Philistines and restoring peace to the land. The chapter concludes with a summary of Samuel's judgeship; clearly it has led to a time of peace for Israel.

Mizpah is a well-known city which serves as a prominent religious and political center in early Israel. It seems to be located just north of Jerusalem, approximately five miles away. Its importance declined during the reigns of David and Solomon, along with the increasing significance of Jerusalem.

The *Ebenezer* mentioned in 7:12 cannot be the Ebenezer of 4:1, since the former site existed long before Samuel erected this monument. The present reference is intended to complete the cycle initiated earlier, since at the 4:1 site, God allowed the ark to be captured, and here God decisively defeats the Philistines. Thus God's work with the Philistines begins and ends at Ebenezer. The etiology of Ebenezer, *stone of help,* suggests that Samuel founded a cultic site here.

The summary in verses 15-17 provides a transition to chapter 8. Many years pass by as Samuel exercises his judgeship, and they are peaceful years. The Philistine threat seems to have diminished, temporarily at least. The Ammonites, the Moabites, and the Edomites are busy attending to matters at home. And internal affairs among the tribes appear to be well managed. As Samuel moves about on his circuit, all Israel profits from his spiritual and political guidance. Ramah, his home, is located in the territory of Benjamin, six miles north of Jerusalem.

Israel's Demand for a King (8:1-22)

Considering Samuel's advancing age, along with the unacceptability of his two sons, the elders of Israel propose to Samuel that he appoint a king as his successor. Samuel's offense at this suggestion reflects his fear that kingship will exact a high price. God instructs Samuel to comply with the elders' request, but to warn them of dangers inherent in kingship. These warnings having been duly issued, the elders reassert their desire for a king. Samuel agrees, but clearly not without misgivings (verses 11-18).

An indefinite period of time has elapsed between 7:17 and 8:1. Samuel has grown older. His sons, Joel and Abijah, are accorded a place in a priestly list in 1 Chronicles 6:28, but here they are pictured as unworthy successors of their father's office. Like Hophni and Phinehas, the sons of Eli, Joel and Abijah are immoral leaders. Their judgeship at Beersheba locates them in a remote part of the territory, at the southernmost tip of

Israel. Possibly Samuel thought their actions would be less conspicuous in Beersheba than elsewhere.

The two reasons cited by the elders in verse 5 are perhaps valid arguments for a change in leadership (Samuel's age and his sons' incompetence), but they must also be understood as part of Israel's belief that an entirely new form of government is needed. The elders want a king to rule Israel, making her like the other nations (verse 20), for reasons of both public ceremony and military efficiency. This material has been written and shaped by a writer who now sees the unhappy consequence of monarchy, and who, as he retells the history when kingship began, depicts troublesome beginnings.

The list of frightful abuses that could be committed by a king comes from a much later time, when the mistakes of kingship have taken their toll (verses 10-18). The writer inserts them here as a forewarning of what might and actually does happen when a king rules over Israel.

The practice of having a male runner accompany the royal chariot was widespread in the ancient Near East. Likewise, the numerical divisions reflect typical patterns of military organization. But conscripted service, common or not, was definitely abusive. Governmental appropriations included an individual's land as well as his wealth, and even his person. Samuel's gloomy forecast portrays almost a picture of slavery, but all to no avail. The elders fail (or refuse) to hear.

So, without bestowing approval, (as in 10:1 and following), God tells Samuel to comply with the elders' request. Perhaps a real hint as to the elders' motives shows in their wish that their king *go out before us and fight our battles* (verse 20). The political situation, in reality, may not have been as tranquil as portrayed in 7:14. Their fear of the Philistines may have prompted a legitimate plea for a new, more effective form of leadership in Israel, but that is not the view of the writer of 1 Samuel 8. For him, the elders' ill-conceived and unjustified request is based on Samuel's age, his sons' incompetence, and Israel's idolatrous wish to be like other nations.

Samuel's Secret Anointing of Saul (9:1–10:16)

Chapter 9 introduces a new perspective into the writer's account of the rise of kingship in early Israel. There are several indications that this section (9:1–10:16) comes from a source other than that of 1 Samuel 8. Samuel, a local seer, is not particularly well-known except as a resident *man of God*. Clearly, he is not the nationally known judge/priest of 7:15. Also, Samuel and God seem to approve of kingship in these chapters, whereas in chapter 8 they both have serious reservations. Many scholars identify the writer's new source here as the pro-monarchy source because of its positive view of kingship. The previous source in chapter 8 resumes at 10:17 and is identified as the anti-monarchy source.

The literary character of this story is delightful. Here we have a classic tale of a journey undertaken for one rather mundane purpose. Suddenly, as if by divine providence, the journey becomes a tale of a special appointment as *prince* over a nation. Even though we are told that Saul is handsome and from an important Benjaminite family, he has no particularly impressive credentials or experiences that would distinguish him for rule over Israel. His own astonishment at Samuel's lavish attention (9:19-20) indicates his complete surprise. Yet, God chooses and empowers Saul, and Samuel anoints him as a prince over God's people. The movement to monarchy has begun.

The reference to Kish and his lineage in 9:1 identifies Saul's family as important (compare Samuel's family in 1:1). Also, that Saul is described as *handsome* (like Joseph, Genesis 39:6) underscores his suitability as a candidate for kingship. There is something very special about Saul.

The missing donkeys supply the outward reason for Saul's journey, but the reader learns very quickly that this trip is to be much more than a search for lost animals. Saul's search for these wayward beasts carries him through the Ephraimite hills, ending in the land of Zuph, Samuel's home territory (1:1), where Ramathaim is located. The suggestion to obtain assistance from a local *man of God* (9:6) is entirely appropriate, since Saul and his companions have exhausted efforts to find the lost donkeys. The expression *man of God* usually identifies a professional holy man, or at least an individual recognized for his powers to discern the divine will. These persons generally receive a fee for their services; hence Saul's initial reluctance. He has no payment for the holy man. At an earlier time in Israelite history the distinction between a *seer* and a *prophet* may have been significant. The term *seer* may have identified those persons who experienced visual revelation, as opposed to those who were singled out by auditory reports and charged with communicating divine messages to other human beings. By this time, however, such differences in the offices are hard to maintain.

The intentional nature of this meeting becomes clear as the reader learns of Samuel's dream the preceding night. Dreams are well-known forms of divine revelation in Israel (Genesis 37:5-11). The real purpose behind Saul's journey becomes apparent at once, as he is God's choice to be the leader of Israel. And Samuel is the divine liaison.

Saul is identified here (9:16) and also in 10:1 as a leader (NIV) or *ruler* (NRSV) (Hebrew *nagid*) rather than as a king (Hebrew *melek*). Most scholars feel that the term refers to the office, *king-designate,* indicating that God has duly appointed and blessed this individual but he has not as yet been publicly installed as king. Divine approval is logically, as well as theologically, prior to popular approval. Saul will be publicly crowned only after he has earned public acclaim following his defeat of Ammon, rescuing the city of Jabesh-gilead (11:1-15). Saul seems to be completely surprised that Samuel knows what is on his mind (9:19), and is even more astonished that Samuel is speaking as he does. After all, Saul exclaims, he is nothing special (9:21). Saul's inclusion in the sacrificial banquet where he receives special portions further disarms him. Finally, as Saul leaves the city, Samuel accompanies him, and at the outskirts he anoints Saul secretly.

The ceremonial act of anointing refers to a special service wherein choice oils or animal fats are placed on the subject's head, consecrating him to divine service. This ceremony means that despite Saul's later rejection as king, he still retains God's earlier blessing. To be anointed as God's servant is a lasting relationship that is not destroyed by human sin. Even David is afraid to harm Saul.

Samuel advises Saul (10:2-13) that God's special choice of him as prince is to be confirmed by three upcoming events: (1) a meeting at Rachel's tomb where Saul is told of Kish's concern, (2) a second meeting where Saul is presented with sacrificial elements, and (3) charismatic endowment. Each of these events unfolds in the manner foretold by Samuel.

In 10:10, we see that God's spirit comes into Saul and he begins prophesying. Receiving God's spirit is known as *charismatic endowment*. In the Old Testament, this gift enables God's leaders (Gideon, Saul, David) to deliver Israel in times of peril. God's spirit empowers a person to perform great acts of heroism. God's spirit aids Saul in battle, just as Saul's leadership diminishes when God withdraws the divine spirit (1 Samuel 15:10; 16:14).

The reference to Saul's newly acquired powers of prophecy is the occasion for a proverbial saying on unusual behavior. People were unaccustomed to Saul acting as he now acted.

The secrecy of Samuel's earlier act of anointing Saul is preserved, even in the face of interrogation by Saul's uncle. The time is not yet right for God's choice to be made known publicly. But certainly the die has been cast. The king-designate is, at least for the moment, a prince.

Saul's Accession—A Second Account (10:17-27)

In sharp contrast to the earlier account of Saul's anointing in 9:1–10:16, the writer now presents a second account of the same event. But differences in detail betray a definite anti-monarchy sentiment, both on the part of God and from Samuel.

Verse 17 resumes the narrative left at 8:22 when Samuel has ordered the people to return to their homes. Samuel has listened attentively to the elders' demand for a king. Ignoring the potential abuses of kingship, the people continue to press Samuel, until finally God orders him to grant their wish and appoint a king. Samuel now responds to God's directive and reassembles the people, presumably the male members of the clans, the tribes, and the families at Mizpah—more than just the elders mentioned in 8:4. Mizpah is one of Samuel's principal sites where he judges Israel. It is located in the Benjaminite hill country, a few miles north of Ramah, Samuel's home.

Prior to the actual selection process, Samuel delivers a stern admonition to his audience from the Lord (verses 18-19). God's words contrast the deliverance of the Israelites from their Egyptian aggressors with their faithless insistence on a king. Nevertheless, God complies with their request, but things may not turn out as Israel expects. As we learned in the ark narrative, God can transform history and bring about unexpected results. Monarchy will not be everything that Israel expects it to be.

The lottery is used in Joshua 7 to discover the violator of God's ban against taking the captured spoils during holy war. Also, it is used by Saul to discover the person who violated his instructions in 1 Samuel 14. Here,

Samuel uses the lottery to choose Israel's new king. This method is particularly appropriate to the task at hand because God, as it was thought, controlled the process and could make the selection. The specific clan to which Saul belongs is called the Matrites (10:21). Little is known about them, since they are mentioned nowhere else in the Old Testament. Once Saul has been selected by the lottery, they learn he is not present. His absence necessitates appealing the matter to God, thereby explaining the etymology of Saul's name, *asked of God*. Samuel inquires of the Lord as to Saul's whereabouts, and the Lord discloses Saul's hiding place. Hence Saul becomes the king who was *asked by the Lord*.

As in the preceding version in 9:1–10:16, Saul is described in flattering terms. His physical attractiveness distinguishes him as special and suitable for a divine purpose. The combination of divine selection and popular acclaim prompt a resounding, if not universal, endorsement by the people: *Long live the king* (verse 24). We can only imagine how disappointed Samuel must feel at this moment, for surely he has given his best effort as a judge, only to be rejected by his people.

The rights and duties of the king that Samuel writes in a book (verse 25) must refer to a manual or administrative guide. We cannot be certain of its content since there is no such document in the Old Testament. Inasmuch as Samuel had grave reservations about kingship in the first place, his instructions probably placed limits on royal powers and protected the fundamental rights of individual citizens.

A king has been chosen, and the popular will has been satisfied, but clearly not everyone feels that Saul can rise to the occasion (verse 27). Whether this reservation toward Saul's leadership is a forewarning of days to come or the momentary grumbling of malcontents cannot be determined.

Saul's Rescue of Jabesh-gilead (11:1-15)

The writer here resumes following his pro-monarchy source, left at 10:16. God's selection of Saul and his secretive anointing at the hands of Saul is now vindicated by a courageous act of deliverance. With the help of a hastily gathered volunteer army, Saul rescues the city of Jabesh-gilead from torture at the hands of the Ammonites. This victory propels Saul into the public eye and distinguishes him as the only viable candidate for king.

The public is unaware that Saul has been approved by the Lord earlier. Thus, the real point of the deliverance at Jabesh is to provide public support for Saul's appointment to kingship. The episode at Jabesh furnishes a clear and convincing answer to the question raised in verse 27, *How can this man* (NRSV; NIV, *fellow) save us?* All doubts are allayed and suspicions removed. Saul is the man of the hour!

Ammon is a small country located northeast of Israel, bordering on or perhaps even overlapping territory claimed by two of the Israelite tribes, Reuben and Gad. It is located immediately east of the Jordan River. Ammon and Israel maintained a seesaw relationship throughout most of their common history, sometimes being staunch allies, but more often being bitter enemies. At this particular moment, Nahash, the Ammonite king, attempts to humiliate the citizens of Jabesh and to render them utterly servile. Seemingly, Jabesh is doomed, having no apparent deliverer at hand. It is little wonder that *all the people wept aloud* (verse 4).

Verse 6 mentions the empowering of Saul by God's spirit, noted earlier in 10:6 and 10:9. This charismatic endowment enabled Israel's earlier leaders, the judges, to perform heroic acts of deliverance. Saul's mighty feats in the present story bear a remarkable, if not intentional, resemblance to narratives of earlier heroes such as Samson, Gideon, and others. At the precise moment of crisis, when all seems lost, God appoints a leader, equips him with power, and miraculously delivers the people. Saul follows in this tradition of Israel's judges, but he seems to be something more as well. Unlike the judges, once the crisis is resolved, Saul accepts his appointment as king, with both God and Samuel in full accord.

The symbolism of the slain oxen is clear: This will happen to your animals unless you participate in the current military relief effort. While Saul's first army is formed in accordance with customary practice in early Israel, he quickly establishes a standing army, complete with skilled leadership and proper training.

Saul attacks Jabesh in the early morning, and catches the Ammonites off guard. The rout is quick and effective. By noon, the battle is over and Saul emerges as the victor. Saul and his army return to Gilgal, and Samuel publicly proclaims him king. God's secret choice now becomes Israel's popular choice.

Samuel's Final Address (12:1-25)

In contrast to the joyful celebration in 11:15 following the public installation of Saul as Israel's king, Samuel delivers a somber speech here in chapter 12. The speech dramatizes the tragic folly Israel has committed in its demand for a king. Most scholars identify this chapter as a continuation of 10:27 (the anti-monarchy source). The entire chapter forms a major climax to this section, concluding Samuel's prophetic leadership and inaugurating rule by monarchy. From Samuel's point of view, however, this new leadership is definitely to be regarded as a form of apostasy. Nevertheless, he will continue to exercise the responsibilities of his office, interceding for Israel and serving as a moral advisor. But his political role is now over, having been passed on to a king.

Samuel begins his final address by eliciting from the people a declaration of his honest and just rule. He has profited in no way at public expense. He has resolved disputes fairly and honestly. He has oppressed no one. Why, then, has he been replaced by a king? Because he is old? No! Because of human sin! Israel's demand for a king is politically unnecessary since Samuel has judged the country competently and successfully. Not even the Lord or an anointed prince can find one single act of dishonesty in Samuel's rule. Is this to be true of the new rulers?

Not only does Samuel find the demand for a king politically unnecessary, but it is also theologically wrong. Verses 6-19 place Israel's present sin in the same context as earlier acts of unfaithfulness. Just as in Joshua 23–24, a leader reminds the people of God's gracious acts of deliverance in times of national distress. In references to God's mighty acts in the Exodus and during the following years of the judges, Israel sinned, and was punished, repented, and was delivered. But now the new sin (monarchy) may be more difficult to absolve. God's appointed judges have great power, and to reject their leadership is a grave mistake. To illustrate just how great is their power, even now Samuel calls upon God to cause a thunderstorm. Suddenly the people realize their grave sin, and stand in fear of both God and Samuel.

Having acknowledged their sin, the people plead with Samuel to continue to serve them and to intercede on their behalf. And although Samuel is still convinced of the evils of kingship, he does agree to continue his responsibilities as intercessor and moral teacher. It is precisely these two functions that distinguish the great prophets of Israel during her later history.

Samuel concludes his address by explaining the nature of divine retribution. Obedience to God's word is met by divine blessing, whereas disobedience generates God's judgment. Even with the dangers inherent in kingship, Israel still can remain faithful and prosperous. The decision is hers.

§ § § § § § §

The Message of 1 Samuel 7–12

Three important theological themes may be found in these chapters: (1) kingship as a form of apostasy, (2) charismatic endowment, and (3) forms of divine guidance.

Samuel's principal objection to kingship is the threat of the sin of apostasy. The first commandment (Exodus 20:3) specifically prohibits the worship of any gods other than the Lord. Generally in the Old Testament, this prohibition pertains to the gods of neighboring tribes who rival Yahweh for Israel's allegiance. But Samuel envisions kingship as a more serious threat. He fears that Israel will deify her monarchs. Israel is a theological community, called by God for special service. Her leaders must stand second to the Lord, not replace the Lord.

Charismatic endowment is the indwelling of God's Spirit. Following his secret anointing, Saul receives God's Spirit (19:6, 9), enabling him to excel in strength, courage, and valor. This same spiritual endowment enlivened the judges, such as Samson and Gideon, and enabled them to perform gallant acts of heroism. The purpose of this gift to God's chosen leaders was to provide leadership at crucial moments in Israelite history, and was an experience that demanded moral accountability.

Throughout the Old Testament, God employs many forms of guidance. The patriarchs and the judges provided leadership for God's people. Now, with the emergence of kingship, God introduces a new form of leadership for Israel. Divine guidance is not limited to priests and prophets, although they play important roles in communicating God's word. Both Saul and David are recipients of God's Spirit. Their successes and failures reflect active divine guidance or punishment.

§ § § § § § §

1 Samuel 13–15

Introduction to These Chapters

With his kingship now formalized, Saul turns his attention toward the immediate threat posed by the Philistines. Evidently, since their previous victory at Aphek (4:10), the Philistines have moved quickly to occupy Israelite territory in the central hill country. Israel's fragile political situation is becoming increasingly uneasy. To complicate matters even further, the Edomites, the Moabites, and the Ammonites are also encroaching upon Israelite soil. Not a moment too soon, Saul initiates a series of bold attacks against Israel's enemies (14:47-48) and stifles, for the moment at least, these aggressors. But Saul's days are filled with warfare and he lives constantly with his boots on his feet.

Here is an outline of these chapters
  I. Escalation of the Philistine Threat (13:1-7a)
 II. Saul's Cultic Offense (13:7b-15a)
III. Israel Against the Philistines (13:15b–14:52)
 IV. A Second Account of Saul's Rejection (15:1-35)

Escalation of the Philistine Threat (13:1-7a)

Verse 1 is an introductory formula used frequently by the writer (1 Kings 14:21) to supply a historical framework for the narratives that follow. During the years of the Divided Kingdom (925 B.C.–722/1 B.C. and 587/6 B.C.), he used a system of cross-referencing the kings of Judah with the kings of Israel (2 Kings 15:32).

But here he indicates Saul's age when he assumed the throne and the length of his reign. Unfortunately both numbers are missing, due to a problem in the transmission of the Hebrew text.

The number indicating the size of the Israelite army in 13:2 and the Philistine army in 13:5 may be approximate rather than an exact head count. The term *thousand* may refer to something like a battalion or a company, to use modern terminology. In comparison with other numbers in the Samuel and Saul stories, these seem small. If, on the other hand, 3,000 is a correct head count, this unit represents a highly select, well-trained unit as opposed to the general muster used by Saul's predecessors.

Verse 3 suggests that Jonathan, Saul's son, stages a minor revolt that catches the larger Philistine army by surprise. This initial success, however, is short-lived when, in verse 5, the Philistines assemble a proper army. Evidently, from the Philistine response, Jonathan's action signals the beginning of open warfare between the tribes of Israel and the Philistines.

The sites of Gibeah of Benjamin, Giba, and Michmash are located close together in the territory a few miles north of Jerusalem. Gilgal is the site where Saul received public confirmation (11:15). The Philistines evidently exercise considerable influence over this region, but their control is now certainly challenged by Jonathan's daring attack. Unfortunately the initial Israelite response turns to outright panic and wholesale desertion in the face of mounting opposition from the Philistines.

The Philistine corp of charioteers certainly must intimidate the poorly equipped Israelites. The sizable contingent of horsemen, along with countless foot soldiers, frightens the Israelites so that they flee into nearby caves and even cross the Jordan. Jonathan's earlier effort now seems totally futile—the Philistines are simply too powerful to oppose. Nothing short of a miracle can rescue Saul, Jonathan, and their beleaguered troops. As they reassemble at Giba, grave doubts must fill their minds. How can they possibly cope with such overwhelming numbers?

Saul's Cultic Offense (13:7b-15a)

In this brief but very significant section, the writer provides an account of Saul's rejection by God, resulting from a violation of priestly prerogatives. In 10:8, Saul is instructed to proceed to Gilgal and await Samuel's arrival in seven days to offer sacrifice. Continuing that sequence of action in 13:8, Saul is here doing precisely as he was told. But Saul's wait for Samuel extends beyond the appointed time, and an alarming sense of panic begins to set in among the Israelite troops. So Saul gathers the offerings and officiates at the sacrificial ceremony himself. No sooner has he finished, than Samuel arrives. When he learns what Saul has done, Samuel reprimands him: This foolish act has offended God. As a result, God will now seek out another man to become king over Israel. Saul's line as king shall not continue.

Close examination of 10:8 and 13:7b-8 indicates that a problem exists with chronology. In 10:8, Saul is a young man who has just been anointed secretly by Samuel. Yet, with almost no description of the intervening years, we find Saul to be a mature adult in 13:7b-8, with grown children (13:3). Complicating matters even further, Israel (including Samuel) has just proclaimed Saul king, and offered peace offerings at Gilgal (11:15).

What led to the events in 13:7b-15 is difficult to determine, but perhaps the description of Jonathan's revolt (13:1-6) followed at a later time the actions in 13:7b-15. These problems notwithstanding, it is at least clear that a major rift occurs at Gilgal between Samuel and Saul. This split seems to mean that although Saul himself will remain king over Israel, his dynasty is not to be established. God will retain the freedom of choice to select a leader.

The three reasons Saul cites (verses 11-12) for performing the sacrifices make good sense. Although the king is not a priest, the Old Testament supplies many examples of kings (including Saul) exercising priestly responsibilities. After all, Saul faced a serious military crisis: The Philistines were about to attack and Saul's army was in a state of disarray. Samuel had not appeared, as agreed upon, in seven days. Saul did not wish to enter battle without God's blessing. Saul even adds that he *felt compelled* (NIV; NRSV, *forced myself)* to proceed with the offerings. He did not act quickly or without thought. He was not consciously attempting to assume privileges not rightfully his own. Unfortunately for Saul, Samuel does not see matters this way.

From Samuel's standpoint, Saul has violated God's command to wait for Samuel (10:8), and has acted presumptuously, usurping privileges usually reserved for priests. This offense angers God. Royal disobedience to divine command does not go unnoticed nor unpunished (12:25). Saul will remain king, but his sons will be without a throne.

Israel Against the Philistines (13:15*b*–14:52)

The Philistine encampment at Michmash is across a wide ravine from Geba, the site of Saul's camp. Evidently this is extremely rough terrain, and the rocky, treacherous cliffs on both sides make good natural barriers. Since the Philistines occupy the higher site, they have a full and relatively complete view of the surrounding territory. To further demonstrate their presence in the region, they send out patrols in different directions. Perhaps this conspicuous presence is a response to Jonathan's preceding assassination. They are not about to let matters get out of hand. Saul's diminished army poses no serious threat to them, so they think.

The reference in 13:19-21 to Philistine control of the iron industry is meant to strengthen the image of a small, weakened, dissipated Israelite army. The list of tools indicates that by this time the Israelites have developed an agricultural economy. The fees charged for servicing the equipment place the Israelites in a position of economic dependency. Even worse, their army is poorly equipped, having no spears or daggers. Surely they are no match for the Philistines.

Jonathan's surprise attack is even more astonishing in view of the imposing terrain. Jonathan devises a plan of attack, predicated on the response of the watchmen. The Philistine guards taunt them, but they seem completely shocked when Jonathan appears. The earthquake causes the Philistines to panic even further (14:15). Saul's troops are aided by Hebrews who seem to have momentarily allied with Philistines, but now reassert their loyalty to their Israelite king. This internal chaos fosters further panic among the Philistines. Their unity falls apart and they begin to flee in every direction (verse 16).

Saul and his troops hear the great commotion across the pass, and discover quickly that Jonathan and a companion are missing. The reference in the Hebrew text to the *ark of God* (verse 18) has been replaced by the *ephod* in the Greek version of this story. Such a replacement is probably correct, since the ark supposedly remained at Kiriath-jearim until David brought it to Jerusalem (2 Samuel 6:1-15). Even as the priest is in the midst of his consultation using the sacred dice (*Urim* and *Thummim*), Saul interrupts him, and hurries off to help his son. The men of Israel gain a great victory over the Philistines this day, but it is the Lord who ultimately insures the win (14:23).

Following the victory at Michmash, Saul institutes a fast for the rest of the day among his soldiers. In all likelihood, Saul's motives are proper. The fast is an appropriate—even if unwise—means of continued presence. Saul realizes that his success to date is the result of divine blessing. Unfortunately, Saul does not anticipate two unforeseen consequences. First, Jonathan is obviously not told of the fast, and he inadvertently consumes wild honey, thereby engendering God's anger and Saul's frustration. Second, the fast leaves Saul's men in a weakened state, so that they forget certain dietary regulations and greedily eat food that has been prepared improperly (verses 31-33). Saul's motives in the case of the ban on food are honorable, but as is so often the case in his life, the consequences turn out different from what he expects. With a weakened army and an alienated son, Saul must now try to reestablish the confidence of his people.

In connection with the fast and the consumption of food that was prepared improperly, the writer includes a reference to Saul erecting an altar to God. In fact, Saul seems to preside over the entire sacrifice, as a priest would. This is especially interesting in light of Samuel's condemnation of Saul in 13:7*b*-15.

When God fails to answer Saul (verse 37), he knows almost immediately that some type of sin has been committed. He summons the priest, who brings the sacred lots, the *Urim* and *Thummim*. Earlier, Saul had been selected king by this same method. Now it is to be used to uncover the one who has violated Saul's ban. A process of elimination follows, and Jonathan is shown to be the guilty party. Saul is prepared to do his duty. Jonathan must die. But the people realize that an honest error has been committed, and Jonathan should be spared. So a substitute offering is provided, and Jonathan, their valiant young leader, is spared.

Verses 47-48 provide a summary of Saul's reign over Israel. War is a constant element during most of his rule, but in this particular narrative, Saul responds to those challenges successfully. The enemies whom Saul conquers all lie close to Israel's borders. There is little doubt that, although Saul's rule lasts only a few years, he succeeds in securing Israel's boundaries. Unfortunately, much of the Saul material has been edited and reshaped by a pro-Davidic writer who depreciated Saul's achievements significantly. Only in a few isolated verses, such as 14:47-48, do we catch a glimpse of Saul's real contributions to Israelite history. In all likelihood, Saul is due much more credit than he receives in the biblical accounts.

An interesting name appears in Saul's family list in verse 49, the name *Ishvi*. The name later appears as *Ish-bosheth* (2 Samuel 2:8) or *Esh-Baal* (1 Chronicles 8:33). Both of the latter names are derogatory, suggesting that the former name, Ishvi, is an editorial change to improve his character. This change would be consistent with the pro-Saul sentiment expressed in this section.

A Second Account of Saul's Rejection (15:1-35)

Chapter 15 is a second account of God's rejection of Saul. But this rejection relates more to Saul himself, whereas the earlier version (13:7*b*-15) announces the termination of Saul's dynasty. The accounts are not contradictory, but instead they complement one another, completing God's denunciation of Saul and his rule over Israel.

Certainly, the Saul of this story contrasts sharply with the Saul of 14:47-48. There, he is the strong, successful military leader of Israel; here, Saul is a weak, easily influenced king, who cowers under Samuel's powerful words of judgment. This chapter describes the unbreachable chasm separating Saul and Samuel (verse 35) that more than justifies the initial reservations Samuel expresses toward kingship. The entire chapter belongs to the anti-monarchy tradition.

Verse 15:1 is a declaration of Samuel's divine

authority. After all, Samuel says, he anointed Saul on God's behalf; now the anointed one must submit to his anointer. Samuel speaks in God's name and conveys God's message, with God's authority. Saul is obliged to listen to him.

The Amalekites are nomadic tribesmen, dwelling mostly to the south of Judah. As the early Israelites were journeying in the Sinai, following their escape from Egypt, they were attacked and harassed by the Amalekites. For this savage assault on God's people (Exodus 17:8-16), God brands them an enemy forever. Thus, Saul's mission is to punish the Amalekites, as God had promised. Even Moses, in Deuteronomy 25:17-19, reminds Israel of God's promise. The act of divine vengeance makes Saul's attack more than mere war; it becomes a holy war. And one of the specific provisions of holy war was a ban on the taking of spoils. All the captured people, their livestock, their possessions, were deemed unclean, and should be destroyed. God would tolerate no profaning of the chosen people by allowing contact with contaminated booty. So Saul's mission is clear. Wipe out the Amalekites.

The Kenites were another nomadic tribe that Israel encountered as she fled Egypt. But this group seems to have been gracious to the Israelites, unlike the Amalekites. So, with due regard, Saul provides the Kenites with ample time to escape the impending attack.

Saul attacks the Amalekites, and in a short time completes his rout. However, he does not follow Samuel's command to destroy them completely (verse 3); instead, he allows the captured king to live, along with the choicest animals. This act of disobedience is in strict violation of holy war. For whatever reasons Saul might adduce later, he has still committed a terrible sin.

Upon learning of Saul's sins (verses 10-12), Samuel grieves over the terrible situation at hand. His worst fears have come true; God's newly appointed king has now sinned by violating God's word. When Samuel confronts Saul, his charge is similar to the indictment he issued in 13:13: Saul has not obeyed God's commandment. The nature of the disobedience is different in this story, but Saul is still guilty of disregarding God's commandment.

Saul cites two reasons for his disobediences: (1) It was the people (not he) who really forswore the ban and took the spoils; and (2) the livestock were to be used as a sacrifice to the Lord. Neither of these reasons is acceptable to Samuel, even if the latter might be true. Reason one is contradicted by 15:9. God's sacrifice must always be of special animals, clean and unblemished, not the contaminated spoils of a hated enemy. Saul's arguments collapse instantly under Samuel's sharp indictment. God prefers obedience rather than sacrifice (verses 23-24). Even if reason one had been true, Saul should have been stronger than to capitulate to the popular cry.

The reference to the *torn hem* is symbolic of God's tearing the kingdom. Samuel has no mercy and extends no forgiveness to a pleading Saul. God's justice may be fair, but it is also stern and uncompromising.

In verse 25, Saul begs Samuel's forgiveness and pleads with the old judge to return to Gilgal with him, as a show of support. Samuel flatly rejects this suggestion (verse 26). Yet, in verse 30, Saul makes the same proposal and Samuel here agrees (verse 31). Possibly there were two accounts of this story.

Samuel fulfills at least part of the holy war ban by slaying Agag, the Amalekite king. The fate of the captured animals remains a mystery.

Samuel and Saul part company, not to meet again until the day before Saul dies. Kingship has not turned out as Israel expected, but it has fared as Samuel feared.

Vindication of this new style of leadership awaits another leader, who will be better than Saul.

§ § § § § § §

The Message of 1 Samuel 13–15

The two prominent theological issues arising within these chapters deal with two human responses to God's word: obedience and disobedience. These opposites form the basis of divine blessing or divine judgment. Saul has received the gift of God's spirit (charismatic endowment), which sanctions his reign as king and strengthens him for extraordinary leadership. Unfortunately, Saul's disobedience causes God to withdraw this blessing and dispense judgment. Samuel's few words on these matters are very insightful into faith and our response.

In 1 Samuel 13:7*b*-15*a*, Saul commits a breach of religious law by usurping priestly functions not available to him: He cultically blesses his army prior to battle, and fails to execute God's orders to destroy completely all of the Amalekites. The fact that Saul's motives are, in both cases, reasonable and appropriate, is beside the point; Saul has disobeyed God's commandments. As consequences of his disobedience, Saul loses his charismatic endowment, loses his claim on the throne of Israel, and loses Samuel's support. These punishments are truly high prices to pay, but Saul's sins are serious. Disobedience to God's word carries severe punishment.

By contrast, obedience to the word of the Lord leads to divine blessing. In fact, Samuel's poignant couplet in 15:22 anticipates the great moral claims of the prophets: *To obey is better than sacrifice.*

§ § § § § § §

PART
FIVE   1 Samuel 16–20

Introduction to These Chapters

Either because Saul usurps powers reserved for priests or because he fails to follow the prescription of holy war, he proves himself an unacceptable leader for the people of God. God rescinds his charismatic endowment. As Saul's successor, God chooses David, the youngest son of Jesse. David's rise to power is filled with dangers and setbacks, but David eventually confirms God's approval and Samuel's anointing. First Samuel 16–20 recounts how this path begins.

Here is an outline of these chapters.

I. God's Choice of David (16:1-13)
II. David's Appointment to Saul's Court (16:14-23)
III. David's Victory over Goliath (17:1-54)
IV. David and Saul's Family (17:55–18:30)
V. Saul's Plot to Kill David (19:1-24)
VI. Jonathan's Help for David (20:1-42)

God's Choice of David (16:1-13)

The writer continues to follow the anti-monarchy source, detailing Samuel's anointing David as Israel's future king. Chronologically, Samuel's selection of David follows immediately upon God's rejection of Saul (15:1-35). One ruler has been rejected, so a new leader must be found. But this task is not easy, since it must be done without Saul's knowledge, and none of the initial seven candidates interviewed are acceptable to Samuel.

Disheartened, Samuel asks Jesse if he has other sons, and he is told there is yet one more son, who is watching the sheep. David appears, and Samuel confirms him instantly as God's choice. Immediately, David is empowered with God's Spirit. Samuel returns to Ramah, his home.

Jesse, David's father (16:1), is listed as a descendant of Ruth and Boaz (Ruth 4:21-22; 1 Chronicles 2:3-12). Evidently Jesse is well-known in Bethlehem, and a man of some wealth, as suggested by the large number of sons. Why Jesse is thus favored by the Lord is unclear.

Bethlehem is a village six or seven miles south of Jerusalem. The elders in Bethlehem tremble (verse 4) because they fear some terrible disaster might befall them at the hand of this holy man.

The selection of God's anointed does not go to the eldest and the most attractive son of Jesse, as might have been expected. Instead, God chooses the youngest son. Like Saul, David is distinguished by a handsome appearance and beautiful eyes, suggesting importance. Not only is David outwardly handsome, but he has an inward quality, discernible by God (16:7). The combination of inward and outward qualities distinguishes David among his peers, and confirms divine approval.

Immediately following Samuel's anointing, David receives God's Spirit, as had previous leaders of God's people. God has withdrawn the charismatic endowment from Saul; now it goes only to one who is *better* (15:28).

David's Appointment to Saul's Court (16:14-23)

The writer begins using the pro-monarchy source at 16:14 and leaves the anti-monarchy source of 16:1-13. No indication is given here of the time elapsed connecting events to 14:52. When God's Spirit is withdrawn, Saul immediately falls into severe depression. His servants summon a young musician/warrior to play for the troubled king, and shortly afterward Saul's mental state improves. David becomes a permanent member of Saul's court, as a musician and armor bearer.

While modern medicine or psychology might explain Saul's illness using different terminology, the Old Testament attributes the king's depression to an evil spirit from God. Just as charismatic endowment empowered Saul to great feats of war earlier, so now does an evil spirit wreak havoc with his mental condition. The depression, prompted initially by his sense of loss of God's spirit, turns to jealousy at David's success. This jealousy then becomes anger, and eventually turns to such hatred that it leads Saul to plot David's death.

David is described in glowing terms as favored by God. But all of the other attributes become subsidiary in comparison to the final characterization, *and the* LORD *is with him* (verse 18). Saul's instant affection for David leads the old king to retain David in his court as a musician and an armor-bearer.

David's glamorous introduction to Saul's court, his personal attractiveness, and his special relationship with God suggest the beginning of a new chapter in Israelite history. The royal mantle will eventually change hands, but not for many days. Saul is a marked man who is clearly in a state of mental, to say nothing of political, decline. David has just begun his march upward. Saul appears to be headed in the opposite direction.

David's Victory Over Goliath (17:1-54)

This section recounts one of the most popular of all biblical stories, how the small but faithful shepherd lad, armed with only a slingshot, slays the mighty giant, Goliath. The classic tale celebrates a universal emotion to pull for the underdog. It also marks the real beginnings of David's meteoric rise to prominence.

From a literary standpoint, the present chapter is a combination of at least two source traditions. There are too many internal elements of disharmony for the chapter to be from a single writer (compare verses 4-9 with verses 23-26). Scholars disagree whether the chapter is a combination of pro-monarchy and anti-monarchy or of unknown sources used by the writer. Also, in certain verses, David appears as a young shepherd lad, unskilled in matters of war and naive in his own strength (32-33). In another account, David (34-36) is an older person, clearly skilled at fighting, even if it is only lions and bears. Complicating matters even further, according to 2 Samuel 21:19, Goliath of Gath was killed by Elhanan, not David.

All of the sites mentioned in verses 1 and 2 are located in Judah. Saul's war with the Philistines has by this time shifted to the south, closer to Philistine territory. As earlier, in the Mizpah battle, the two opposing armies align themselves on hills, separated by a valley. Confrontation usually occurs when armies or individual representatives come down off the respective hills to do battle.

Goliath of Gath is identified as a Philistine warrior (verse 4). He stands over six and one-half feet in height (assuming a cubit is about eighteen inches and a span is six inches) and is equipped from head to toe with the finest armor. He is seemingly invincible. Moreover, he is ruthless and mean. Goliath taunts the smaller, less properly attired Israelites with challenges to do battle. It is little wonder that he strikes fear into the hearts of Saul's veteran soldiers.

Supplying soldiers with food was a very common practice in ancient Near Eastern warfare, particularly among nomadic tribes where there was no central government. Once a man's sons were drafted by means of a general muster, it became his responsibility to provide them with food and equipment. Hence, Jesse sends David with provisions for his brothers. Evidently David is too young to join the army. He belongs at home with his family, tending sheep (verse 28). This tradition reflects no knowledge of David as Saul's royal musician/armor bearer.

David is outraged and offended at Goliath's taunts, and immediately volunteers to battle the giant. Saul hesitates to allow this inexperienced young lad to challenge a veteran soldier, but finally agrees when he sees and hears David's resolute determination (verses 34-37). At first, David outfits himself with Saul's armor, but quickly finds that he can barely move. So he sets it aside and goes forth, armed only with a sling and five small pebbles. Clearly David's inexperience and inadequate equipment mandate divine assistance. But David is convinced that God will deliver him and aid him, just as before. He is not afraid.

Goliath is insulted that little David is the best Israel has to send forth into combat, and he is also amused that such an unlikely foe has the nerve to meet him. His remarks about him being merely a *dog* reflect the notion that dogs were detestable creatures. Goliath has been publicly demeaned. He fully intends to carve this brash Hebrew into small pieces.

David attacks Goliath at the only vulnerable place in his armor—his forehead. When the giant collapses, David runs up, seizes his sword, and cuts off Goliath's head. The Philistines see their champion cut down and beheaded, and they immediately panic and flee homeward.

David and Saul's Family (17:55–18:30)

In the three verses (17:55-58) at the end of chapter 17 David is introduced to King Saul. Strangely, this event seems to occur just before David goes up to confront Goliath. Having slain the giant (verse 57), David returns and meets Saul, apparently for the first time. Obviously, this section contradicts 17:1-54, especially verses 31-35. Abner is presented again (compare 14:50) as the commander of Saul's army. Perhaps this incident follows verse 30. Although it is difficult to assign this brief episode to a source or to a proper chronological place, the emphasis on David's career as a military leader is clear.

Almost immediately, as David enters Saul's service, the popular young warrior develops a warm friendship with Jonathan, Saul's son. In fact, this relation proves to be one of the strongest bonds between any two persons in the Old Testament. There is trust, respect, and genuine affection between David and Jonathan, to such an extent that Jonathan willingly bestows upon David has own robe, armor, bow, and girdle. These gifts not only signify friendship, but acknowledge David's future kingship. They formalize this relationship by means of a covenant (18:3).

The real power and significance of God's withdrawal of Saul's charismatic endowment begins to emerge now. Saul, having been abandoned by God, is beset with jealousy, and begins plotting David's death. Yet, at every instance, he is foiled in his attempts, seemingly by God's protective hand. On the other hand, David, having received God's spirit, experiences one success after another. It is little wonder that the writer indicates that Saul was *still more afraid of* David (verse 29).

David's marriage to Michal is clearly more than a romantic relationship. Saul views the marriage as a likely way to rid himself of a threat. There is no way David can produce a hundred foreskins from the Philistines without getting killed. David sees the marriage as a future claim on Saul's throne. Neither motive justifies marriage!

Through all of David's exploits and his rise to fame in Israel, God stands with him. The writer leaves no doubt as to the ultimate reason for David's mighty acts. Nor can there be any doubt about Saul's complete frustration. God controls history.

Saul's Plot to Kill David (19:1-24)

The friendship between Jonathan and David (see 18:1-4) now prompts Jonathan to try and persuade Saul not to have David killed. He suggests two reasons to Saul for restraint: (1) David has done nothing to Saul personally to anger him, and (2) David has distinguished himself with expert military service. Saul's actions would only bring bloodguilt upon himself for slaying an innocent man. Saul seems to agree with Jonathan's reasoning, and, for the moment, abandons plans to kill David.

The exact chronology of verses 11-17 is difficult to determine. The reference to *that day* might be either to David's wedding day (18:27) or to the day when Saul himself almost killed David (19:8-10). We can imagine that, since Saul's motive for offering Michal to David as his wife was only a plot anyway, only a short period of time has elapsed since the wedding. David escapes through a window, adjacent to the city wall. Presumably the house where he and Michal live is built alongside the city wall, so that none of the soldiers guarding their home can see him escape.

The word *idol (teraphim)* refers to a small idol or family god. Michal uses the family god to fake David's presence. She lies to Saul to protect herself, knowing her father's anger. Truly, this is remarkable loyalty.

The final story in this chapter seems to belong to an independent source. The pro-monarchy source has already provided an account of the origin of this proverb (10:10-12). The anti-monarchy source says Saul and Samuel never meet again until after Samuel's death (15:35). Here the story functions in two ways: (1) It reestablishes a connection between Samuel and David, and (2) it inaugurates Saul's unsuccessful pursuit of David. In this version of the saying, Saul's unusual ecstatic behavior points ahead to further strange acts of a man who is torn apart by jealousy, anger, and frustration. Saul's unstable mental condition, once a private matter, is now public.

Naioth may have been a section in Ramah where prophets assembled.

Jonathan's Help for David (20:1-42)

Chapter 20 records a separate version of the breakup between Saul and David, which seems inconsistent at several places with the stories in chapter 19. Here, David still dines regularly with Saul at Gibeah. He knows of Saul's plots to kill him but does not understand the reasons. Further, there is no reference to Michal as David flees. The writer has integrated an independent source into his narrative at this point, to serve two purposes: (1) to reiterate the complete breakup of Saul and David, and (2) to provide a rationale for David's gracious kindness to Jonathan's son, Mephibosheth, in 2 Samuel 9:1-7.

This narrative opens with David coming to Jonathan, hoping to learn the reasons for Saul's recent attempts to kill him. Initially, Jonathan cannot believe that his father feels this way (compare 19:1-7), but eventually he is convinced and agrees to help David. They devise a plan whereby David misses a monthly feast at Saul's table, and the king's reaction (presumably as a sign from God) indicates his *real* feelings for David. Jonathan then is to communicate Saul's attitude by a prearranged signal.

The renewal of the covenant bonds of friendship between Jonathan and David forms an important section of this chapter. This covenant outweighs Jonathan's loyalty even to Saul.

David's prolonged absence from Saul's table prompts the king to inquire as to his whereabouts. Jonathan's explanation about David's attendance at a family feast at Bethlehem evokes Saul's rage. Saul accuses his son of conspiracy and humiliates him before the assembly at his table. Saul further indicates that he does not really understand Jonathan's part in this treason, since by his very actions, he undermines his own claim to Saul's throne (verse 31). Since Jonathan does not know what his friendship with David is doing, Saul must act for him, and eliminate the threat to his dynasty. David must be killed.

§ § § § § § §

The Message of 1 Samuel 16–20

The two themes in these chapters that are the most significant, theologically, are: (1) God saves by faith, not by sword or spear (17:46); and (2) ecstatic behavior of prophets (19:24).

The story of David and Goliath illustrates the universal literary motif of the weak humiliating the strong. But David is more than merely a weak man; he is a man of God. He is absolutely confident that the Lord, through him, can destroy this pagan adversary. David's strength, therefore, comes from his faith in the Lord rather than in military weaponry or combat experience. The message is clear: God's people need to put their faith (trust) in the Lord, not in things of war. This faith brings a power that is even stronger than giants. Israel needed to hear this message, and, like David, draw her strength from the Lord.

When David slips away from Saul by night, he flees to Samuel and the prophets at Ramah (19:18-24). Saul sends his messengers to retrieve David, but the messengers fall victim to the spell of God's spirit and begin to prophesy. The same experience befalls the messengers a second and a third time. Finally, Saul himself goes in search of David, and finds himself subject to the same spiritual endowment and its resulting unusual behavior. Saul disrobes and immediately begins to prophesy.

Manifestation of religious zeal in the Old Testament has long been identified with the phenomenon of prophecy. God's spirit frequently caused its recipients to act in unusual ways (see Ezekiel 37:1-4).

§ § § § § § §

1 Samuel 21–24

Introduction to These Chapters

From the national prominence and acclaim as Saul's celebrated warrior, David has to flee for his life. He becomes a fugitive overnight. Saul pursues David with an unrelenting vengeance that is fueled by paranoia and by an evil spirit from the Lord. Humor and pathos permeate these narratives, and they represent excellent examples of ancient Israelite literature.

Here is an outline of these chapters.

David's Escape to the Priest at Nob (21:1-9)

Continuing the narrative of the pro-monarchy source, the writer records an episode involving David and Ahimelech, a priest at Nob. This story seems to follow directly the report of David's escape from Saul's palace, aided by Michal, in 19:11-17. His hasty departure from his bedroom chamber contrasts sharply with his carefully planned escape in chapter 20.

Immediately, David goes to Nob in order to secure food and weapons, having left Gibeah too quickly to gather supplies. At first, Ahimelech hesitates to comply with David's request, but soon he acquiesces, believing David's reassurances. The entire incident is witnessed by a certain Doeg the Edomite, who eventually betrays David and even serves as executioner for the priests at Nob. The entire story illustrates that even David is not above acts of outright deception in his quest for the throne.

Ahimelech (21:1) is a distant relative of Eli (1 Samuel 1–3). His current service as priest at Nob serves to link Abiathar (22:20) to David and justify David's great kindness to his family.

The cultic center at Nob apparently enjoyed prominence at this time, owing mainly to the departure of the ark from Shiloh. Nob is located a few miles south of Gibeah.

Ahimelech's initial fear of David is well founded. Ahimelech must have thought it strange that David would appear, alone, asking for food and weapons. After all, David was a soldier in Saul's army and would have access to regular food and arms. How is it that he appears now requesting provisions? Unfortunately, David misrepresents his motives for the visit and deceives the priest.

David indicates that he is on a special mission, of a highly secretive nature. He is to meet his soldiers, shortly, and needs food. The only food available, Ahimelech explains, is the Holy Bread of Presence. This is a ceremonial food used in religious worship. It is therefore sacred, and can be eaten only under conditions of cultic purity and in the context of worship. More usually, this bread is eaten by the priest as it is removed from the altar and replaced on the sabbath by hot bread.

On the one hand, David's explanation is patently false. He does not wish the food to feed men engaged in holy war (thereby cultically pure), but he wishes to eat it himself as he flees from Saul. During holy war, soldiers are to refrain from all sexual activity, since their mission is considered sacred. Therefore, David reassures Ahimelech that his men are *clean*. But the New Testament writers excused David by explaining that cultic requirements may be set aside to meet human need (Matthew 12:3-4). Other than the holy bread and Goliath's sword (21:9), Ahimelech performs no service for David.

Doeg the Edomite has presumably remained at Nob for some type of religious rite of purification. The expression *shepherds* (verse 7) may refer more to a military position than to a pastoral responsibility. He appears later (22:9) as an informer and in 22:18 as the executioner of the priests at Nob. Both of these deeds are more appropriate to a soldier than to a shepherd. Whatever his function in Saul's court, Doeg is an evil character.

Goliath's sword last appeared in 17:54, where it was hidden in David's tent. It is unclear how it was removed to the sanctuary at Nob.

The *ephod* (21:9) refers to a chest of some cultic significance rather than to a garment (14:3). This may be the ephod (23:6) that contained the sacred dice used in obtaining oracles from the Lord. In the absence of the ark, perhaps the ephod distinguished Nob as a major cultic site in early Israel.

David's Move to Gath (21:10-15)

Three brief incidents (21:10–22:5) interrupt the unity of the Nob stories. The first account reports David's visit to Achish at Gath. Second, he returns to Adullam, close to Bethlehem, and finally he relocates his parents to Mizpeh, a city in Moab. In his almost frantic efforts to escape Saul, David runs from place to place, seeking support and protection.

David first flees to Gath, a Philistine city approximately twenty miles southwest of Jerusalem. David's motive for visiting Gath might have been to offer his services as a soldier (as in chapter 29), or to seek asylum from Saul. At any rate, he is recognized almost instantly as a famous soldier, whose exploits are celebrated in verse. With his identity exposed and his life in danger, David resorts to dramatics. He pretends to be insane and fools everyone, Achish included. Since insanity is thought to stem from demonic possession, Achish and his followers let the demented warrior alone.

The reference to David as *king of the land* indicates the Philistine belief that David was a local ruler. He was clearly well known, but not yet equal in rank to Saul. This title is more a term of respect than a designation of political leadership.

David Moves on to Adullam (22:1-5)

David next moves to the stronghold located at Adullam. The word *cave* (22:1) is better translated as a fortress or stronghold. This important military fortification appears again in 2 Samuel 23:13-14 as David's base of operations.

Adullam is located approximately fifteen miles southwest of Jerusalem. Here, David is in, or is at least close to, his home territory. Accordingly, his family rallies about him both for support and for protection. Also, David attracts a host of supporters who represent socially, economically, and politically disenfranchised elements of society. These persons are refugees of one sort or another, who seize an opportunity to alleviate their distress and to punish the systems which rejected them. Thus David's earliest support comes from his family and from an odd assemblage of malcontents. Out of this group, David creates an army.

While he is hiding at Adullam, David relocates his parents to a safer location in Moab, a territory immediately east of Judah, across the Jordan River. The exact location of Mizpeh has not been determined.

David's choice of Moab as a haven reflects his lineage back to Ruth, a Moabite woman, to whom he was related distantly (great-grandmother; see Ruth 4:13-22). David does not know what God has in store for him (22:3). The forest of Hereth cannot be identified.

Saul's Massacre of the Priests at Nob (22:6-23)

This story begins with a typical image in ancient literature of a tribal chieftain seated beneath a tree, holding council with his subordinates (see Genesis 18:1). The tamarisk tree denotes royalty. Saul has evidently learned that David has escaped, with help from Jonathan and others. Saul reminds them that they may expect little or nothing from David in the way of gifts or preferential military treatment. These rewards will go to southern Judahites, not to northern Israelites.

Then Saul tries to play on their guilt by indicating that they did not disclose to him the covenant between David and Jonathan. Saul uses intense rhetoric in his paranoia, and spares no words to achieve his desired purpose. But interestingly enough, Doeg, an Edomite (a non-Israelite) speaks up and supplies Saul with information, some of which was not reported in the earlier account (21:1-9). Nowhere does Ahimelech consult the Lord on David's behalf in the earlier version. Also, the reference Saul makes to stirring up his servant against him is unclear; we have heard nothing of a rebellion against Saul up to this time. Doeg seems only too ready to expose Ahimelech.

When Saul summons Ahimelech and all the priests of Nob, he begins questioning them as to why they have aided and abetted a fugitive. Ahimelech pleads complete ignorance of the break between Saul and his former servant, David. As for the intercession, the priest indicates that on many previous occasions he has inquired of the Lord on David's behalf. Ahimelech pleads ignorance; he knows nothing of matters at Gibeah. This argument makes good sense. But Saul's anger is so great that he refuses to believe Ahimelech and orders the immediate execution of all the priests.

Saul is not a rational man. Since the priests are deemed holy to the Lord, Saul's servants are afraid of divine reprisals, and they refuse to obey the frantic king. But Doeg, as earlier, accepts his king's bidding, and proceeds to lead a slaughter, killing not only the priests, but all the inhabitants of Nob as well. As a non-Israelite, he is not afraid of Israel's God. The priestly center is completely destroyed, save for one son of Ahimelech, who escapes to David. His name is Abiathar.

David welcomes Abiathar, and extends him protection. But David also acknowledges his part in this tragic massacre. David now adds a priest to his company, strengthening his ties to the Lord.

Saul has now completely severed all forms of communication with God. He has alienated Samuel to the point where they no longer speak. God has withdrawn the charismatic endowment. Saul is now alone, and his obsession with David hurls him toward a disastrous end.

David's Stay at Keilah (23:1-13)

With a priest now at his side, David has strengthened his channels of communication to the Lord. In the episode at Keilah, the writer continues following the pro-monarchy source, although we see some internal tensions. Why, when David consults the Lord in verses 1-5, does he not use Abiathar and the sacred ephod? Also, how is the ungrateful attitude of the Keilah citizens to be explained, just after David frees them from Philistine raiders (verse 12)? Perhaps the two sections (verses 1-5 and 6-13) were originally separate units. They were combined because of the common site, Keilah, with which they dealt.

David appears here as an unofficial overlord for cities in Judah. Keilah lies just a few miles south of his fortress at Adullam. The city seems to be under attack from the

Philistines, who are even foraging their cattle on the remains of Keilah's threshing floor. David's men are reluctant to leave the safety of Adullam, and agree to assist Keilah only after David has received assurance from the Lord that they will be victorious. It is interesting that despite Abiathar's presence David does not employ the sacred ephod until later. Perhaps verse 6 should be placed before verse 4. Keilah is freed and the Philistine cattle are captured. The Lord has spoken properly to David.

Word reaches Saul that David is at Keilah, and Saul immediately sets out to kill him. Since the city has walls and gates, and the windows have bars, Saul plans to trap David inside. But David learns of Saul's plans and sends quickly for Abiathar, the priest, and the sacred ephod. The ephod is a small chest containing the sacred Urim and Thummim. Through the priest David consults the Lord with questions which may be answered yes or no: Yes, Saul is coming to Keilah; and yes, the men of Keilah will turn David over to Saul. So David and his men (now up to 600) scatter in every direction, and Saul halts his expedition.

With a priest at hand, David can come to no harm. Without a priest, Saul is doomed to failure. And so it will go until Saul finally meets his tragic death.

David's Reluctance to Kill Saul (23:14–24:22)

David's efforts to avoid Saul require considerable travel throughout the Judean wilderness. He moves from his fortress at Adullam south to the Wilderness of Ziph, then further south to Maon, and finally over to the cliffs surrounding the spring at Engedi. Several times Saul almost captures him. He is betrayed by the Ziphites, a Judean tribe David probably thought loyal to him. Finally, he demonstrates great wisdom and restraint by cutting off only a small piece of Saul's royal robe when he has the opportunity to eliminate him altogether.

Confronting Saul with his innocence, David swears an oath to pay Saul's line due regard. But Saul has to acknowledge that David is to be his successor, just as had Jonathan, earlier. This pro-Davidic writer leaves no doubt that David pays proper homage to Saul, is innocent of any wrongdoing, and certainly retains clean hands in the death of God's anointed king. With God's blessings, David remains guiltless. Saul, on the other hand, finds himself constantly frustrated in his efforts to protect his throne and secure his dynasty.

The Wilderness of Ziph is a rocky, desolate region in the Judean hill country south of Hebron. We are not told why David and his men leave the safety of Adullam. Perhaps David thinks he can count on support from his fellow Judahites. Perhaps he is on an undisclosed rescue mission or a fee-collecting trip for protection offered the citizens. We are simply uncertain as to David's motive.

The brief report of Jonathan's visit reconfirms the covenant these two friends sealed earlier (20:8). Jonathan offers David encouragement and assures him that his father will not harm him. But more importantly, Jonathan acknowledges that David is to be Israel's next king. All he wishes is to be second in command. Saul also knows this, Jonathan says.

The report to Saul from the Ziphites that David is hiding in their territory indicates that Saul still has considerable support, even in Judah, David's home region. Saul's area of control far exceeded the Benjaminite hills north of Jerusalem. But just before Saul arrives, David escapes further south to Maon. As David attempts to avoid capture, owing to excellent military tactics on Saul's part, he finds himself squeezed in a pincer movement, as Saul's men surround the hill where he is camped. Only Saul's hasty and ill-timed retreat, to counter a Philistine raid, spares David certain capture. In fact, this place became known as the Rock of Escape (verse 28).

The spring at Engedi was an important water source in early Israel. The spring lies just west of the Dead Sea, and joins rapidly ascending cliffs. It is rugged and treacherous territory, punctuated by numerous caves. As the name *Wildgoats' Rocks* suggests, some parts of this territory are unfit for human habitation, then as well as now. Either by chance or by divine providence, Saul turns aside and enters a cave. As it happens, this is the very cave where David and his men are hiding. David's men urge their leader to seize this opportunity to end their days as refugees, and kill Saul. But David resists their council and contents himself with cutting off a small piece of Saul's skirt. Truly, David exercises great restraint, as the temptation (and pressure) must have been great. But Saul, however demented he may have become, is still God's anointed; therefore, he is sacred and not to be touched. David's hands remain clean.

When Saul leaves the cave, David follows him and confronts him. David explains that he has spared Saul's life, has no malice in his heart, and is not guilty of treason. David even swears an oath of innocence. He cannot do Saul harm, for wickedness only comes from a wicked heart, which David does not possess. God is a witness to David's righteousness.

Saul listens to David and responds by acknowledging his own guilt. He concedes that David has done him no harm, even though he had opportunity. More importantly, Saul openly declares David to be the future king, requesting only that David preserve his family. David agrees, and both men part company. Saul returns to Gibeah and David returns to Adullam.

§ § § § § § §

The Message of 1 Samuel 20–24

Two important theological issues emerge from studying 1 Samuel 21–24: (1) Human needs take priority over religious regulation, and (2) reverence is to be shown the servants of God.

In 21:1-6, David deceives Ahimelech, a priest at Nob, into providing him with food and weapons. Ostensibly, David has embarked on a secret mission and requires help from Ahimelech for himself and his men. Actually, however, David wants the supplies for himself, as he flees from Saul. Also, David appropriates holy bread, usually reserved for the priests. David must escape Saul's assassination plot, and he must secure food before fleeing to safety. Thus David's misconduct is a necessary step in avoiding death at the hands of Saul. Human needs clearly take priority over the regulations of cultic law. In the New Testament, three of the Gospel writers include the story of Jesus plucking grain on the sabbath (Matthew 12:1-14; Mark 2:23–3:6; Luke 6:1-11), placing human need above the sabbath laws. Jesus even invokes David's actions in the Nob incident as precedent for his own behavior. Hungry people cannot hear the word of God—on the sabbath or at any other time.

The second major theological theme in these chapters is reverence for the servants of God. Such individuals, whether they are prophets, priests, or kings, are considered sacrosanct. David offers sanctuary to Abiathar, the refugee priest from Nob; he avoids killing Saul, God's anointed king. David almost always uses the priests to consult the Lord prior to military activity. He handles the ark with great care when he brings the sacred object into Jerusalem. David shows respect for God's servants.

§ § § § § § §

PART SEVEN 1 Samuel 25–31

Introduction to These Chapters

This section is bracketed by the deaths of two important leaders in early Israelite history, Samuel (25:1) and Saul (31:4).

Here is an outline of these chapters.

David's Courtship of Abigail (25:1-44)

The opening verse of chapter 25 is a notice of Samuel's death. In view of Samuel's national fame and prominence, the brevity of the remark is surprising. This notice is repeated in 28:3, to set the scene for Saul's seance with Samuel.

This delightful story tells how David acquires two members of his harem, Abigail and Ahinoam. The writer here resumes the pro-monarchy source left at 23:14 following David's escape at Keilah. David is the leader of a renegade band of soldiers, and furnishes protection to local land owners in return for payment. David appears to have left his fortress at Adullam, and is currently operating in the area close to Hebron—namely, the regions of Ziph and Maon.

Verse 1b states that David went to the Wilderness of Paran; this reading follows the Hebrew text. The Greek version reads *Maon*, as in verse 2. Due to the considerable distance of Paran from Maon, as well as from Ziph, the Greek reading seems more appropriate.

Nabal, whose name means *foolish*, is a wealthy shepherd who belongs to the Calebite tribe (Numbers 13; 14). Unfortunately, he has a mean disposition.

The scene opens with Nabal conducting a sheep-shearing festival which is partly work and partly celebration. David has been serving as a protector for Nabal and for his valuable flocks. David doubtless served also in a similar capacity for other residents of the area. But when David asks politely for provisions as payment for his service, Nabal refuses and asks, "Who is the son of Jesse?" The reference to *many servants* who are *breaking away* indicates the turbulent and uneasy political situation in Judah at this time, hosting frequent raids from the Philistines, the Amalekites, and others. David's sense of outrage (verse 13) is understandable, considering Nabal's insult.

One of Nabal's servants describes the dangerous situation to Abigail. Probably he fears for his own life, and hopes proper intercession can be made. The servant verifies David's claim that Nabal's possessions have in fact remained safe and undisturbed under his protection. Thus Nabal's response is not only insulting to David, but also unjustified. David's threat (verse 22) must strike terror into the hearts of Nabal's servants.

Abigail responds by hastily gathering lavish provisions and sending them immediately to David, following shortly behind herself. Her gracious and courteous manner impresses David greatly. She argues that David should reconsider his threat and should do no harm to Nabal. After all, the man is a fool, as his name implies. David needs to remain guiltless before God and not stoop to this act of revenge. She reminds David that his life is closely guarded by God (verse 29) and that Nabal poses no serious threat to him. Therefore he must not take matters into his own hands, and replace God by slaying Nabal himself, for this act would usurp the prerogative of God (verses 28-31). This was precisely Saul's sin when he blessed the troops at Gilgal (13:8-9). Bloodguilt is inappropriate for Israel's next king.

David agrees to her proposal and accepts her gifts. Abigail returns home. At the proper moment, she tells Nabal. Almost instantly, he suffers a fatal stroke (verse 37) and dies shortly afterwards. David then proposes marriage to Abigail, and she accepts. David has acquired not only a beautiful and intelligent wife, but considerable wealth and land as well. He has extended his influence in the southern territory of Judah. Further strengthening his ties in the south, he marries another princess from Jezreel, a Judahite (not a northern) city, Ahinoam by name. By this time, Saul has already given Michal, David's first wife, to another man. Once again, divine providence has halted David from making a tragic mistake, and has rewarded him with a perfectly suited mate.

David Spares Saul a Second Time (26:1-25)

Still following the pro-monarchy source, the writer presents a second version of the Ziphite betrayal and David's refusal to take Saul's life. As in the 23:19-25 account, the Ziphites inform Saul as to David's whereabouts in their territory. But due to excellent intelligence information, David learns of Saul's plan, and even the site of his encampment (verses 4-5). Just as in the 23:19 account, David is residing at Hachilah in Jeshimon, a region in Judah, close to Hebron. Some commentators suggest that the two versions of this incident may be different accounts of the very same event.

David's army doubtless counted many foreigners among its numbers, such as Ahimilech, a Hittite (not to be confused with Ahimelech, the priest at Nob, 21:1-6). The Hittites occupied the modern country of Turkey, and during the 15th and 14th centuries B.C. found their way southward into Canaan. In fact, Canaan served as a battleground for warfare between the Hittites and the Egyptians during the 15th century. This prolonged struggle left many Canaanite cities (such as Jericho) destroyed or at least weakened and defenseless to nomadic raiders.

Zeiuah (verse 6) is David's sister (1 Chronicles 2:16), the mother of Abishai and Joab. Abishai and David sneak into Saul's camp at night, when everyone is sleeping, including even Abner, Saul's major general. Discovering Saul unprotected, Abishai urges David to seize the opportunity God has seemingly given him and to slay the king. But David resists temptation, as earlier. David then explains that Saul's fate should be left in God's hands (verse 10).

David and Abishai content themselves with stealing only a spear and a flask of water to prove they were really there. The deep sleep which has fallen upon Saul and his troops, preventing them from awakening at David's intrusion, is no accident. God has caused it.

David crosses the valley and stands atop the mountain opposite Saul's camp. He shouts to Abner, accusing him of dereliction of duty. Saul awakens at the sound of David's voice, and recognizes him immediately. David then testifies to Saul that he has committed no wrong against the king. He does not understand why Saul thus pursues him. If God has condemned David to Saul, then sacrifices must be offered to atone for David's guilt. But if men are the source of Saul's angry pursuits, then these men should be cursed for their lies and for depriving David of his rightful inheritance from Saul.

In either case, David pleads for his life and asks Saul to

abandon his relentless hunt (verse 20). Saul admits then that David is truly innocent and that the guilt lies with him. David reminds Saul that he has spared his life, and would like the same treatment. Saul agrees, and they part company on seemingly friendly terms. They never meet one another again. Saul's farewell includes no reference to David's future kingship, as did the earlier version of this story. Saul merely wishes David well.

David's Service to the Philistines (27:1–28:2)

Chapter 27 is a detailed version of David's defection to Achish, the Philistine king of Gath. A briefer and somewhat different version of this meeting appears in 21:10-15.

David's voluntary enlistment in Philistine service might be considered treason by some persons. After all, Saul spent most of his reign fighting Philistine aggression; the Philistines were the enemy. Perhaps Achish is now ready to accept David's offer, seeing the advantage of David's large, well-trained army. In the earlier story, David was a recent fugitive from Saul, with only a few followers. Now he could be of real service to Achish. David would make a better ally than an enemy.

It is difficult to detect David's motives. Perhaps he is severely depressed and troubled by Saul's seemingly relentless pursuit. Possibly he is truly afraid for his safety and for that of his family. It is clear, however, that at no point during his tenure at Ziklag does David battle his own people. So in this sense, David retains his loyalty to the people of God. The expression *said in his heart* (NRSV) means *thought to himself* (NIV).

In return for his military service, Achish grants David a territory that he may claim as home, the city of Ziklag. This site is located deep in the south just on the edge of a line between Philistia and Judah. It strengthens David's hold on southern territory and provides him a base of operations.

Fortunately, Ziklag is located sufficiently far from Gath that David can conduct operations without close scrutiny from Achish and his fellow Judahites by raiding tribes hostile to Judah, while claiming to be pillaging Judahite tribes. The Geshurites and Girzites are tribes not well known to us in the Old Testament. The Amalakites are traditional enemies of Israel, with whom Saul has had hostile relations previously (1 Samuel 15).

Since David leaves no survivors after his attacks, there is no one to dispute his claims. The regions David tells Achish he raids are located also in southern Judah, but they are fellow Judahites and therefore kinsmen of David.

David is so successful in this deception that Achish promotes David to a rank of permanent bodyguard. Fortunately, events occur in such a way that David is able to preserve Achish's trust without compromising his loyalty to Judah and to God. He continues this charade for sixteen months. He avoids Saul and strengthens his ties to Judah, both under the nose of Achish, an enemy king. David is shrewd.

Saul Meets with Samuel's Spirit (28:3-25)

The brief notice of Samuel's death (verse 3) and his burial at Ramah repeats information provided earlier in 25:1a. Here, however, it introduces a story involving Saul's use of a medium to consult a deceased Samuel. The writer is reminding us that Samuel has already died; therefore Samuel must resort to extreme (and illegal) measures to establish contact.

Commentators suggest that this chapter interrupted the stories about the Philistine war to prepare for David's revenge against the Amalekites (chapter 30).

Shunem and Gilboa are high hills that oppose one another across the Valley of Jezreel.

Mediums and *wizards* (NRSV; NIV, *spiritists*) refer to the diviners who used different means to communicate with the spirit world. Such practices were specifically forbidden by law (Leviticus 19:31; 20:6). Saul has even expelled them for practicing their apostasy in Israel. The medium's fear of Saul's reprisals make her reluctant to perform her service, until she receives sufficient assurances that she will not be punished. Symptomatic of his desperation at the moment, Saul violates his own decree in order to contact Samuel. He is truly desperate for guidance.

The three forms of revelation mentioned in verse 6 are traditional ways of communicating with God. However, since Saul has offended God and slaughtered all the priests, he finds himself alone. Further conveying the sinister atmosphere of the hour, Saul disguises himself and proceeds at night. Truly, this is a pathetic scene, with the great king sneaking around at night in frantic search for a soothsayer.

Samuel is called upon from Sheol, the place of the dead. In ancient Hebrew thought, it was a dark and dreary place where deceased persons went and slept. No distinctions existed in Sheol. All persons, regardless of earthly standing, went there.

How the medium realizes that it is King Saul who has come to her, based on the apparition of Samuel, is unclear. Some commentators change *Samuel* to *Saul* in verse 12 to resolve this problem. The substitution requires reading the *saw* (verse 12) as meaning that she looks more closely at the man making the request, thereby enabling her to recognize her petitioner as Saul.

In verse 13, she says she sees a *spirit* (NIV; NRSV *divine being)* coming up out of the earth. The Hebrew word *elohim,* or *god,* may be more properly translated as *spirit.* These spirits who resided in Sheol were thought to have special knowledge of future events. This belief may be part of the reason these spirits were taboo in Israelite society.

Samuel angrily confronts Saul with four dreadful announcements: (1) God is about to take away Saul's kingdom; (2) God is about to turn Saul's kingdom over to David; (3) Saul will experience defeat by the Philistines tomorrow; and (4) Saul will die tomorrow.

Saul faints not only for lack of food but out of absolute terror. The announcements of Samuel probably confirm the tormented king's worst suspicions. Only after lengthy pleading by Saul's servant and the frightened medium does Saul arise. He eats and leaves with a sense of resignation. Saul is guilty of disobedience and he must now suffer the consequences.

David's Dismissal from Service (29:1-11)

Chapter 29 continues the narrative interruptive at 28:2 by Saul's experience at Endor. David has thoroughly convinced Achish, the Philistine ruler of Gath, that he is loyal and trustworthy. So successful is David's deception that achish appoints him as his permanent bodyguard. Here, the Philistine army assembles in preparation for a major military offensive against Saul. As the troops march by, the Philistine commander observes David and his troops accompanying Achish. Instantly, they criticize Achish for bringing along David, and demand that he be sent home. Achish is forced to dismiss David tactfully, and send him back to Ziklag while they march northward to meet Saul.

The location of the Philistine encampment here at Aphek suggests that this episode precedes the events of chapter 28, where they are said to be at Shunem, preparing for battle. These sites are approximately fifty miles apart. Shunem is located opposite Mount Gilboa, across the valley of Jezreel. Aphek is in Ephraim, northwest of Jerusalem, on the coastal plain.

In the Philistine military parade the foreign mercenaries accompany the lords to which they are pledged. David and his troops are with Achish. But he is recognized quickly as being the famous warrior of King Saul.

Achish's reasons for including David in the battle fall on deaf ears. The Philistine commanders offer the following reasons for dismissing David: (1) He could turn against them, in favor of his own people; (2) he could not justify his disloyalty to Saul; and (3) he is too popular and too dangerous.

Achish's tact in telling David that he must return to Ziklag and not participate is truly remarkable. The phrase *fight against the enemies of my lord the king* may refer either to Achish or to Saul. Divine providence has spared David the embarrassment of fighting against his own people. At the same time, David's clever deception remains secure. God maintains sovereign control over human history, and does not allow a future king to sin. David's so-called defection to the Philistines is, in effect, a brilliant maneuver. It allows him to avoid Saul and await God's actions in this matter, and it enables him to ingratiate himself further with his Judahite kinsmen.

David's Revenge on the Amalekites (30:1-31)

Here is a brief interlude about David's revenge against the Amalekites. While the Philistine armies are northward in the valley of Jezreel, preparing for battle with Saul, the Amalekites seize the opportunity to conduct forays against defenseless Philistine and Judahite cities. Even David's city, Ziklag, is touched, and its citizens are taken captive.

The Amalekite raiders probably took advantage of Philistine absence to pillage some of the smaller cities and territories. Also, they have suffered from Israelite hands on more than one occasion. They were probably going to make slaves of the Ziklag captives, hence they spared their lives. These semi-nomadic raiders from far to the south of Judah are the epitome of evil in the Old Testament.

David demonstrates his faith once again (23:6) by consulting God by means of Abiathar, the priest, and the sacred ephod. The ephod is the small chest containing the sacred Urim and Thummim. God gives him the go-ahead and promises him victory. David will not retaliate without divine sanction.

David and his men must be very tired following their three-day march of about fifty miles from Aphek (verse 1). But now they must arise and go forth in pursuit of the Amalekites. Some of the men can travel only part of the way (verses 9-10), and stop to rest at Besor. They also are probably weak from hunger, not finding much food left in Ziklag.

As they hasten after the Amalekites, David and his troops come upon a stranded Egyptian. This poor fellow has been an Amalekite slave, but due to his untimely illness he has been deserted and left to die. He agrees to guide David to the Amalekites in return for food and protection.

Having defeated the Amalekites and released the captives, David seizes the spoils of war, including much pillage that had been stolen from other cities. As David divides these prizes, some of his troops wish to exclude those soldiers who have not participated directly in the battle. But David displays great justice, and divides the spoils evenly. He also ingratiates himself to the elders of Judah by sharing further the spoils of his successful raid.

David is laying a foundation for his future assumption of kingship. This practice set a legal precedent in Israelite warfare. The spoils belong to all members of the group, regardless of their level of participation. These gifts came from God, not from human effort. Obviously David gains political advantage as well, since the Judahite chieftain realizes that he is still *their* protector and not a traitor to the Philistines.

Saul's Death (31:1-13)

The very next day, following Saul's experience at Endor, a major battle occurs between Israel and the Philistines. Not surprisingly, Israel is defeated soundly, with Saul's three sons all dying. The old king himself is badly wounded, and pleads with his servant to finish the job, thereby sparing him further torture or humiliation. But the servant refuses. So Saul does the deed himself.

The Philistines discover the bodies of Saul and his sons, and hang them out for public view in Beth-shan. Remembering Saul's kindness earlier in his reign, the men of Jabesh-gilead slip into Beth-shan at night and remove the bodies for proper burial.

Evidently the Philistine defeat of Saul's army is thorough. They even cross the valley of Jezreel and attack his troops in their camp atop Mount Gilboa. The valley of Jezreel is an important agricultural region in Israel, and is also the location of a major road through the mountains. Caravans passing through to Egypt almost always had to pass along this road. The valley is enclosed by Beth-shan to the east and Megiddo to the west.

With this defeat, the Philistines control most of the cities of the north, and the tribes of Israel are now destitute of significant leadership. Their army is in disarray. Their king is dead. Their cities are occupied. Matters must appear rather gloomy. Although Abner and Ishbosheth establish a small government in exile, they are powerless against the Philistines.

Saul's armor bearer refuses in verse 4 to kill the king, for he is still God's anointed servant. So Saul does the grim deed himself. Suicide is an act not viewed with favor within the Old Testament, and it clearly attests to Saul's complete alienation from God.

Cremation was not a typical practice, and in the version of this incident in 1 Chronicles 10:12, Saul's bones are buried, not burned. Many religious superstitions surround the handling of deceased bodies in ancient Israel, and one's tenure in Sheol could be disrupted by improper burial. Although Saul is, even up to the end, God's duly anointed servant, he dies an uneremonious death.

With Saul's death, the history of Israel's first king concludes. It has not been an entirely satisfactory experience, either for Saul or for the people who so enthusiastically pressed Samuel for a king. Saul, almost from the start, is a man beset with personal doubts and fears. He has serious disagreements with Samuel. He is jealous of David. He constantly does battle with the Philistines. He feels completely alienated from God.

Yet Saul's reign does have some positive elements. He does manage to bring some sense of unity to Israel, and he does garner the support of many tribes both in the north and in the south. Saul also successfully checks the Philistine invasion, at least up until the final battle. But despite these few successes, Saul's reign is pale beside those of David and Solomon. And since much of his reign is described by a pro-Davidic writer, we must not expect an unbiased history. We shall probably never know the real Saul.

§ § § § § § §

The Message of 1 Samuel 25–31

Three issues emerge from studying 1 Samuel 25–31:
(1) Divine guidance of the affairs of history, (2) the many
forms of divine revelation, and (3) justice among God's
people.

David was open to divine guidance. He has good
reason to avenge Nabal's insult, yet he listens to
Abigail's wise words urging restraint. She tells him to
avoid incurring bloodguilt and that God, not David, will
take care of Nabal. In a second incident, David refuses to
allow Abishai to kill Saul, and explains that God will
deal with the king. And, David consults the Lord in the
matter of revenge against the Amalekites (30:7). David's
faith in soliciting divine guidance distinguishes him from
King Saul.

There are many forms of divine revelation. In 28:6-7
Saul seeks a word from the Lord by three traditional
forms of revelation in the Old Testament: (1) dreams
(Genesis 37:5-11), (2) casting of lots (1 Samuel 14:41), and
(3) prophets (Amos 3:7). These are all acceptable types of
solicitation of the divine will.

There is justice among the people of God. Following
David's successful retaliation against the Amalekites
(Chapter 30), he is urged to limit the spoils to the men
who participated actively in the effort. David refuses,
and insists that all his soldiers share in the prizes of
victory (30:24), regardless of their level of involvement.
In fact, David even extends his generosity to other tribal
leaders of Judah as well. David's actions reflect his belief
that it is God who gives him victory, not his own military
might. Therefore, these prizes of war belong to God, and
ought to be divided fairly among all of the people of God.

§ § § § § § §

2 Samuel 1–4

Introduction to These Chapters

The opening four chapters in 2 Samuel cover events
from Saul's death to the assassination of Ishbosheth, his
son. Between these two deaths, much of importance
occurs for David, for Judah, and for Israel.

Most of the literary problems that occurred in
1 Samuel are absent in 2 Samuel. Although the writer
does employ different sources, he harmonizes them in
such a way as to produce a continuous narrative of
David's reign.

Here is an outline of these chapters.

   I. David Mourns Saul and Jonathan (1:1-27)
  II. David's Reign at Hebron (2:1-11)
 III. Abner's Killing of Asahel (2:12-32)
 IV. Abner's Defection to David (3:1-39)
  V. Ishbosheth's Murder (4:1-12)

David Mourns Saul and Jonathan (1:1-27)

Commentators are divided on the relationship of this
chapter to 1 Samuel 30 and 31 because it presents a
different version of Saul's death. The earlier version in
1 Samuel 31 records that Saul took his own life, after
being wounded by Philistine archers. But here there is no
mention that he is injured, the archers are replaced by
Philistine chariots and horsemen, and Saul dies at the
hand of an Amalekite. Perhaps the Amalekite is lying in
order to win David's approval. Given David's dislike for
the Amalekites, the young man's lies make sense.

Unfortunately, there is no hint in the Bible that the Amalekite is lying. For now, the tension between the two accounts must remain unresolved. In verse 2, the appearance of the Amalekite reflects authentic signs of mourning. David and his men soon join the public lament (verse 11-12), and their collective voices weep for the slain heroes. If we assume that the Amalekite has falsified the details of Saul's death, then his appearance is probably not genuine.

The young messenger identifies himself to David as an Amalekite (verse 13), the son of a sojourner in Israel. Residents of non-Israelite ancestry are known as sojourners, or resident aliens. They are protected by law, granted certain rights, and are accountable for certain responsibilities. There is no indication that this man served in Saul's army, so we cannot be certain what he was doing atop Mount Gilboa, if not scavenging for spoils. He brings David two items from Saul that suggest David is to become the new king. Instead of being rewarded for his efforts (or lies), the Amalekite is killed for committing a sacrilege against God's anointed king. Even a sojourner in Israel should have known better than to commit such an act of murder.

Throughout the stories of David's years as a fugitive from Saul, the writer emphasizes David's restraint from harming Saul. David passed up two opportunities to kill Saul. Here again David's hands remain clean. He executes Saul's assassin, proclaims a day of mourning and fasting, and offers a eulogy to the slain heroes.

David's lament over Saul and Jonathan (verses 19-27) is an excellent example of early Hebrew poetry. Both in style and content this hymn is classic. The imagery of the mighty but now fallen warrior is graphic and repeated for emphasis (verses 19, 25, 27). Persons are warned not to mention these deaths in the Philistine camps, so that the unclean enemy may not boast of victory. Mount Gilboa, the scene of this great tragedy, is cursed into desolation, for it now harbors the desecrated shield of Saul. Yet there is still cause for pride amid the sorrow of the day. Saul and Jonathan were mighty warriors, whose weapons distinguished them in battle. Both Saul and Jonathan receive proper accolades from David, who displays his affection for both men. The tone and pathos of David's words for Jonathan remind us of the close friendship between these two men.

David's Reign at Hebron (2:1-11)

Following Saul's death, David turns to the Lord to determine what he is now to do. The Lord instructs him to proceed to Hebron, where he is crowned king. Meanwhile Abner, Saul's general, has escaped death at Mount Gilboa, and has fled to safety across the Jordan River to Mahanaim. Accompanying Abner is Ishbosheth, Saul's youngest son. Together, these two men establish a government in exile.

Hebron is a large city, approximately twenty miles south of Jerusalem. It is the center of the region of Judah. David has strong family and political ties to this area by virtue of marriages to Abigail and Ahinoam, and because he shared the spoils of war with the tribal leaders (1 Samuel 30:26). Perhaps they are the same men who received these gifts earlier. David relocates his entire household to Hebron, suggesting that this move is permanent.

David then moves quickly to recognize and reward the men of Jabesh-gilead for their heroism in removing the bodies of Saul and Jonathan. Also, David indicates that he would be receptive to their loyalty, now that Saul is dead. To win the loyalty of Jabesh would give David an important foothold in Israelite territory, now under the rule of Saul's general, Abner, and Ishbosheth.

The city of Mahanaim lies in Gilead, across the Jordan River. Since the Philistines now control Saul's kingdom, west of the Jordan, the remainder of Saul's house must seek refuge elsewhere, east of the Jordan. Saul's son,

Ishbosheth, is only a small boy and is dependent on Abner for co-regency. As indicated in 1 Chronicles 8:33 and 9:39, the name *Ish-Bosheth* has been changed from *Ishbaal*, to delete any reference to an Israelite king being named after a Canaanite god (*Ishbaal-man of baal*). Elsewhere, the same person is called *Ishvi* (1 Samuel 14:49). As it now stands, Ish-Bosheth means *name of shame*. He is a weak and ineffective ruler, haunted by suspicions of Abner's quest for power.

The numbers mentioned for Ish-Bosheth's age (40 years) and for the length of his reign at Mahanaim (2 years) and David's reign at Hebron (7 years) are all problematic. Given Abner's real power over Ishbosheth, it is doubtful that Saul's son was much older than a child. Also, the years the two men reigned are doubtful, in view of subsequent events in chapters 3 and 4. We are not certain of the length of their reigns, but they certainly lasted long enough for general fatigue to begin to set in (3:1).

Abner's Killing of Asahel (2:12-32)

With David now anointed as king of Judah, and Abner and Ishbosheth struggling to retain Saul's kingdom from their exile at Mahanaim, a clash between these two forces is inevitable.

In verse 12, Abner and his young, possibly untrained army leave Mahanaim, possibly in reaction to David's gestures toward Jabesh (2:5-7). They can hardly afford to concede additional territory, since the Philistines now control most of the central and northern hill country. It is unclear from the biblical account whether the encounter with Joab and David's troops is by design or by accident. Gibeon is a very important city in Israel, six miles south of Jerusalem, and one whose residents might have remembered with bitterness Saul's earlier efforts to terminate them (2 Samuel 21:1-9). Joab could not have chosen a friendlier site to confront Abner, if strategy played a role in this encounter.

The contest (verse 14) proposed by Abner may have

been a game of some type, or it may have been representative warfare. (The Hebrew expression in verse 14 may imply more than a sporting contest. The exact nature of the contest is unclear.) Matters progress quickly to an all-out battle, with Joab clearly emerging as the victor (verse 17). In fact, the section of Gibeon where this incident occurred received the name *Helkath-hazzurim, field of flight*. The exact meaning of this word is unclear, but it designates the site of serious warfare.

To avoid allowing the leader to escape, Asahel, Joab's brother, follows Abner with unrelenting determination. He presses forward, leaving Abner no choice but to stop him. And so he does, by a blow so hard that the butt of Abner's sword strikes Asahel and goes all the way through his body. Asahel may have been fleet of foot, but his bravado exceeded his abilities. And this mistake proved more costly than he could have imagined.

Almost immediately, Asahel's two brothers take up the pursuit of Abner. But Abner assembles his forces atop a hill, and begins negotiations to end the chase. Abner pleads with Joab to stop this vengeance before more blood is spilled. After all, this hostility exists only because matters went too far in the contest at Gibeon. No one else needs to die, he says. Joab listens, and agrees. He ends the pursuit, and both parties return to their respective homes.

Arabah is the desert region south of the Dead Sea extending to the Gulf of Aqabah. It can also refer to the larger basin between the Sea of Galilee and the Dead Sea, as it does here. Abner and his troops are marching north toward Mahanaim, having just left Gibeon.

This episode lays the foundation for future hostilities between these two generals. Joab has reasons of bloodguilt to hold against Abner. But further, when David appears on the verge of a deal with Abner, in return for his defection from Ishbosheth, Joab has professional reasons for hating Abner, as well. These two help explain Joab's brutal attack on Abner in 3:30.

Abner's Defection to David (3:1-39)

The purposes of 2 Samuel 3:1-39 are twofold: (1) to legitimize and authorize David's assumption of power over Israel, and (2) to exonerate David of any guilt in the deaths of Abner and Ishbosheth. David prefers to leave this punishment up to God.

The chapter begins with a brief summary of the military situation between Israel and Judah during the closing years of the eleventh century B.C. Since Saul's death, Israel and Judah have been at war almost constantly. Although the Philistines appear to control some of the major cities in central Palestine, including the cities bracketing the Esdraelon Valley, Abner still commands the tribes of Benjamin and Ephraim, and the Transjordan region. Ishbosheth's tiny government-in-exile continues to grow weaker from this conflict, while David's rule grows stronger.

The insertion of verses 2-5 clearly interrupts the continuous narrative about Israel's and Judah's warfare. The list of David's sons is interesting, but out of place here. Other than establishing royal residency at Hebron, the list is of only statistical value.

Ishbosheth's charge that Abner has misappropriated one of Saul's concubines amounts to treason. Whether it is an accusation based on fact, the narrator does not say. Ishbosheth may have grown frightened at Abner's increasing power (verse 6), and he may have felt threatened. His wish would be only to curb Abner's prominence. Or the charge may have been real, and Abners himself had manifested designs on Ishbosheth's throne by his action. At any rate, Abner is outraged. He immediately begins negotiations with David to defect, bringing all Israel with him.

David's condition for accepting Abner's defection is the return of Michal, his first wife. David had obtained her hand in marriage, at a sizable cost—the foreskins of two hundred Philistines (1 Samuel 18:27). But he was forced to leave Michal in order to avoid Saul. Later, Saul gave Michal to a man by the name of Palti (1 Samuel 25:44). Now, to reestablish his legitimate claim to Saul's throne, David requests that Michal be taken from Palti and given back to him. A frightened Ishbosheth is only too glad to comply with David's demand—or possibly he is too weak to decline.

In 17-19, Abner confers with the elders of Israel regarding the coming defection to David. Particularly noteworthy is his direct and personal contact with the Benjaminites. Since Saul was from this tribe, they could possibly have harbored the most objection to David. But all the elders in Israel agree. David should be king. The agreement is presented to David by Abner and a feast is held (verse 20) to commemorate the covenant. Abner and David then part company on friendly terms (he went *in peace*, verse 21).

When Joab returns from a raid, conspicuously scheduled to coincide with Abner's visit, he learns Abner and David have met and parted peaceably. Suspicious of Abner's motive, Joab warns David that Abner is gathering intelligence that might prove dangerous. Unknown to David, Joab summons Abner, and brutally murders him (verse 27). With a stroke of his sword, Joab satisfies his need for revenge and eliminates a rival for David's favor. But David reacts in horror to the news of Abner's death (verses 28-29). He is clearly upset by the sheer brutality of Joab's act. But he is also disturbed about the potentially dangerous political effects. How would the elders of Israel receive this news? Would they wish him to become king? So David goes to great lengths to prove he has absolutely nothing to do with Abner's murder. He places a terrible curse on Joab's house (verse 29) that includes (1) a continual bodily discharge, (2) leprosy, (3) effeminacy, (4) death by violent means, and

(5) impoverishment. Also, he orders a day of mourning and offers a lament over the slain warrior (verse 33). David spares no expense in exonerating himself from Joab's act. But as for punishing his nephew, he leaves that to the Lord (verse 39).

Ishbosheth's Murder (4:1-12)

With Abner dead, Ishbosheth is absolutely distraught, knowing that he is no match for David. A sense of national panic grips Israel. Who will deliver them from the Philistines? Certainly not Ish-Bosheth! Two of his own soldiers slip into the royal palace in Mahanaim, as the unguarded king lies sleeping, and assassinate Ishbosheth. Expecting to gain favor from David, they bring him Ishbosheth's head. But, as in the instance of the Amalekite's news of Saul and Jonathan, David reacts with anger. He has the assassins killed, and has Ishbosheth's head buried at Hebron, in the tomb with Abner.

The identification of Ish-Bosheth's murderer as coming from the tribe of Benjamin (verse 2) is interesting, since Saul himself belonged to this tribe. The national desperation must have cut deep into Israelite hearts, even into the heart of the young king's own tribe. Even they know that David must become king.

An editorial note (verses 2-3) explains how native Benjaminites came to occupy a non-Israelite city (Beeroth). Originally, Beeroth was occupied by the Beerothites, but they fled during a purge by Saul as part of his hostilities toward the Gibeonites (2 Samuel 21:1). Native Benjaminites then settled in Beeroth.

The insertion (verse 4) is out of place in this narrative. A later editor may have wished to remind readers that, even though Saul's line was about to end, there remained a descendant upon whom David would show kindness (2 Samuel 9). The name *Maphibosheth* may have been changed from *Meri-baal* (1 Chronicles 8:34) for the same reason Ish-Bosheth's name was changed from Ishbaal.

§ § § § § § §

The Message of 2 Samuel 1–4

Two important issues arise in these four chapters:
(1) Proper and improper motives for punishment, and (2)
the nature of David's faith.
There are proper and improper motives for
punishment. When Abner must, for reasons of
self-defence, slay Asahel, he incurs the bloodguilt
obligation from Joab and Asishai. Their motive in taking
Abner's life is clearly revenge (3:7). Yet, what Abner does
is a matter of necessity. He does not plot Asahel's
assassination, nor brutally stalk him out of malice. He
even tries to persuade him to abandon his pursuit.
But Joab, on the other hand, seems motivated by
jealousy. His crime against Abner is a mean and
despicable act that is beyond even David's capacity to
punish. Unprovoked vengeance is truly an unacceptable
motive for punishment. The Lord may excuse revenge as
a reprisal for clearly criminal behavior, but Joab clearly
goes too far in this case.
David's faith in God is of a special nature. David's
faith in the Lord manifests itself in several actions that
combine creed and conduct. David always consults the
Lord prior to a major decision. He allows the Lord to
exercise leadership. Second, David respects the Lord's
prerogatives in dealing with evil. He avoids taking the
lives of Saul and Joab, even though he has sufficient
reason. Third, he has a profound respect for human life,
and refrains from taking it whenever possible. Life is
sacred and must be honored.
David's faith serves as an appropriate model for
persons today who are struggling to discover what it
means to live according to God's will.

§ § § § § § §

2 Samuel 5–8

Introduction to These Chapters

In 2 Samuel 5–8, David keeps his rendezvous with destiny. Ishbosheth is now dead and there are no further hindrances to block his ascendancy to the throne. The elders of Israel come to Hebron and anoint David as their king, and the United Monarchy is formed. This united nation will last for almost three-quarters of a century (about 1000 until 922 B.C.), until it breaks apart during the early months of Rehoboam's (Solomon's son) reign.

Here is an outline of these chapters.

I. David's Rule over All Israel (5:1-16)
II. David's War Against the Philistines (5:17-25)
III. David's Transfer of the Ark to Jerusalem (6:1-23)
IV. God's Covenant with David (7:1-29)
V. David's Military Conquests (8:1-18)

David's Rule over All Israel (5:1-16)

With the death of Ishbosheth, David becomes the only viable alternative to assume the throne of Israel. Recognizing this situation, the elders waste no time in journeying to Hebron, where they anoint David as their king. David's first official act as a ruler of all Israel (north and south) is to capture the Jebusite fortress at Jerusalem, and name it as his new capital. Hiram, king of Tyre, acknowledges David as the new ruler of Israel, and provides timbers for building a royal palace. Finally, there is a brief note identifying the sons born to David at Jerusalem.

Most commentators recognize duplicate accounts of David's enlistment as king of Israel. Verses 1-2, together with 4-5, form an expansion of the original statement in verse 3. Clearly there are discrepancies in the two versions: the first account (actually a later account) has: (1) all the tribes of Israel visiting David (verse 1), (2) references to family ties (verse 1), and (3) references to an anonymous pronouncement of the Lord concerning David's future leadership (verse 2). This elaborate version contrasts with the brief account in verse 3. In neither account does David initiate their visit, nor is there a reference to any earlier agreement supposedly negotiated by Abner (3:17-19).

The numbers used in reference to David's age and his length of reign may be exaggerated to indicate a long time. Solomon (1 Kings 11:42) is also alleged to have reigned forty years.

The reference in verse 2 to the Lord's announcement that David is to shepherd his people has no clear reference in the preceding narratives. The allusion is fitting for someone with David's pastoral background. Also, the terms of the covenant are not disclosed. Probably, the elders agree to supply David with personnel and supplies in return for leadership and protection. The nature and limits of his authority over his subjects remain unclear.

The account of David's capture of Jerusalem has textual problems in the original Hebrew and obscure terminology. It is difficult to reconstruct exactly how he accomplished this takeover, but the scholarly consensus is that Joab and a small contingent of David's own private soldiers slipped into the city by way of the water conduit, and surprised the Jebusites.

Jerusalem was a very old city, dating back to the 15th century. According to Joshua 15:63 (see also Judges 1:21), the invading Israelites under Joshua could not conquer Jerusalem during their conquest in the thirteenth century. The city remained in Jebusite hands until David's time.

The *blind and the lame* (verse 6) refers to the residents' belief that little resistance will be needed to ward off an attack from David. Further references to David hating these persons suggests that David will tolerate no interference, not even from supposedly weak (or unclean) persons.

Jerusalem is a perfect choice for David's new capital. It is located midway between Israel and Judah, thereby offending neither group. It is located on a high elevation, surrounded by valleys on three sides, offering safety from attack. And the city is politically neutral, having been occupied by Jebusites rather than Hebrews.

The Millo (verse 9 NRSV; NIV, *supporting terraces)* refers to a certain section within Jerusalem. It seems to have something to do with a landfill of some type, either like a rampart or a raised mound for some purpose. There is also a reference to the Millo in 1 Kings 9:15, 24.

The reference to King Hiram of Tyre constructing a royal palace for David is misplaced, chronologically. Unless there were two Tyrian kings with the same name, this Hiram is also the one who supplied timbers to Solomon for the Temple in Jerusalem many years later (1 Kings 5).

Tyre was an important coastal town in Phoenicia that flourished at approximately the same time as Israel. The region surrounding Tyre was world-famous for its quality lumber, particularly cedar.

The list of David's sons born in Jerusalem contrasts with the earlier list of the ones born at Hebron (3:2-3). A concubine was a female slave who provided sexual service to her master, but did not have the same rights and privileges as a wife.

David has a very large family, and the issue of succession will not be easily resolved. With so many heirs, jealousy and rivalry are bound to fracture domestic harmony in David's palace.

David's War Against the Philistines (5:17-25)

The Philistines quickly perceive David as a threat to their position in Canaan, for a unified Israel poses a more serious challenge than a separated Israel and Judah. Adding to their concern, David, a powerful military leader with whom they are already well acquainted, is now the new king of all Israel. Their feats are well grounded, for as soon as Israel and Judah unite under David the Philistines begin losing their authority over Canaan. Shortly David will drive them from Israelite territory and confine them to a small region along the southwestern coast.

Many commentators suggest that this text is out of place chronologically. They suggest that these two battles occurred prior to David's capture of Jerusalem. In fact, they insist, David's capture of Jerusalem is precisely what triggers the Philistine attack. But other scholars argue that Jerusalem falls to David after he eliminates the Philistine menace. The *stronghold* in verse 17 refers to David's earlier fortress at Adullam.

Baal-perazim (verse 20) is a play on words referring to the site of David's initial encounters with the Philistines. The words translate *lord of perazim*. It is thought to be located 10-15 miles southwest of Jerusalem. When David names the present site Baal-perazim, he makes a pun meaning that the Lord has broken through enemy lines here, as a torrent of water bursts through a wall. In other words, the Lord has opened a hole in the Philistine armor.

The defeated Philistines flee for their lives, leaving even their idols (verse 21) for David and his men. To capture the religious objects of an enemy represents a decisive victory. Recall the celebration when the Philistines captured Israel's ark at the battle of Ebenezer (1 Samuel 5).

Just as he has opened himself to divine guidance previously, David asks the Lord for counsel regarding these two battles. God approves, and even suggests a certain military tactic. When David hears the rustling of the trees (verse 24), this is to be understood as a sign of the Lord's presence, and David should advance immediately. David does as the Lord commands and gains a great victory that day.

From Geba (NRSV; NIV, *Gibeoa*) *to Gezer* indicates the sizable territory regained by David as a consequence of these two battles. Geba is a city approximately six miles north of Jerusalem, in Benjaminite territory. Gezer is about 18 miles west of Geba, on the edge of Philistine territory. Both of these cities had originally been a part of Saul's kingdom, but were lost to the Philistines. Now, David brings them back into Israelite hands. More importantly, Philistine power has begun to wane in Israel. Their ironclad grip has been loosened.

David's Transfer of the Ark to Jerusalem (6:1-23)

Thirty thousand (6:1) means thirty units. The writer uses thousands and hundreds to designate military units. We cannot be certain of the number of men comprising a thousand. The many participants in this procession signify its great importance.

Baale-judah (6:2) is probably another name for Kiriath-jearim (Joshua 15:9, 10). When we last heard of the ark, it had been carried to Kiriath-jearim, to the house of Abinadab. His son, Eleazar, assumed responsibility for the sacred object. Apparently, Abinadab has two other sons, Uzzah and Ahio (or possibly *his brother*). There is no reference here to Eleazar, unless Uzzah is an alternative form of the name Eleazar.

The procession bearing the sacred ark to Jerusalem has all the markings of a religious celebration, as would be expected for an object of this importance. The ark rests on a new cart, suitable because of its purity and lack of contamination. But, the procession is abruptly halted as it nears Jerusalem. Although the Hebrew text is unclear as to the details, the oxen pulling the cart stumbles, almost dislodging the ark. When Uzzah tries to steady the ark, he grasps the sides of the chest. Alternative explanations have the cart merely tilting, or Uzzah himself stumbling. Angry at being touched by unclean hands, the Lord strikes Uzzah and kills him. Fearing God's anger, David disbands the procession and places the ark in the home of a certain Obed-edom.

Obed-edom is identified as a Gittite, a man from Gath. Since his earlier days as a Philistine mercenary in the service of Achish, David has maintained strong ties to Gath. Later, he is served by a host of mercenaries from Gath, led by Ittai (2 Samuel 15:19). These Gittites exhibit great loyalty to David.

Finally, three months later, David safely resumes the procession into Jerusalem and into the fortified section properly called the City of David. The march culminates in a religious celebration, led by David himself, clad in priestly garb—a linen ephod (verse 14). All along the road, David offers many sacrifices (verse 13). Once in Jerusalem, he continues making burnt offerings and peace offerings. It is permissible for David to perform these offerings because, at this stage, priestly duties are generally limited to obtaining oracles and bestowing formal blessings. All the residents share a common meal, commemorating this occasion.

However, Michal, David's wife, takes offense at David's enthusiastic behavior (verse 16) and reprimands him for humiliating her in public and making a spectacle of himself. Apart from David's being scantily clothed, we cannot be certain what sorts of actions Michal finds offensive. But David is angered by her remarks and reminds her that God chose and placed him in this position as king. Even the servants hold him in more respect than does Michal. He then sends he away, and forever denies her access to his chambers. The line of Saul's family now has no possibilities of continuation, but with David so firmly in control, he does not need the sanction of Saul's descendant in his court.

God's Covenant with David (7:1-29)

Chapter 7 explains why David does not (or is not allowed to) build the Temple. Within the chapter there are some tensions: (1) Why does Nathan originally support David's plan, issue a priestly blessing, and then suddenly change his mind following a word from God? (2) Why does God express disdain for a house proposed by David only to anticipate one built by David's son (verse 13)? (3) How could Nathan, a prophet, have misunderstood God's will, originally? These problems suggest that the entire chapter has a complicated and lengthy literary history. As it now stands in the story of David, God's covenant with David provides a theological sanction for kingship and points forward to the construction of the Jerusalem Temple by King Solomon.

Nathan, the prophet, is introduced here for the first time (verse 2). Generally, court prophets served as royal advisors, frequently soliciting oracles from God and providing God with a mouthpiece to the king. Nathan appears on several occasions with the Bathsheba affair (2 Samuel 11) and the appointment of Solomon (1 Kings 1–2) as David's successor.

In the present passage, Nathan initially sanctions David's plan. But, after receiving a disapproving word from the Lord, he changes his mind about the project. His formula for delivering God's message—*Thus says the* LORD—is a standard form of prophetic speech in the Old Testament. Although Nathan is a member of David's court and therefore likely supported by David, he is no royal lackey. When properly authorized (or provoked), he can issue the king a divine reprimand.

Nathan's oracle to David contains two principal points: (1) God is offended that David has proposed to build a house, having neither asked for one nor felt the need for one. (2) Instead, God will provide David a *house*, meaning a dynasty. Furthermore, God intends to see that David's name is celebrated and praised as one of the great kings of the earth. And God will provide a measure of rest and peace for David and Israel.

On the basis of this famous oracle, leadership of God's people is now to be determined by dynastic succession. God promises never to withdraw from David's house. Besides the present explanation, two other reasons are given in the Old Testament for David's not building the Temple: (1) 1 Kings 5:3 suggests that David was too busy, and (2) 1 Chronicles 22:8 mentions David's active participation in war.

David's response is a sincerely stated prayer of appreciation of God's special grace toward him. David acknowledges that any accomplishments he may have had (or may have in the future) come solely from God. Like Israel, David has been selected for greatness and blessed because of divine grace. David's prayer concludes with a request that God continue to look with favor and grace on David and upon all his descendants. This prayer is a superb model of faith and piety.

David's Military Conquests (8:1-18)

The Philistine menace is silenced here, once and for all (verse 1). The writer provides a complete account of these battles in 2 Samuel 21:15-22 and 23:8-39. The city retaken by David, Methegammah, may refer to Gath (1 Chronicles 18:1). However, some commentators prefer to change the vowels in the Hebrew text and treat Methegammah as if it referred to a region rather than to a city.

Moab is a small nation directly east of the Jordan River from Israel. Earlier (1 Samuel 22:3), David had sought protection for his parents in Moab, based on blood ties back to Ruth and Boaz. But apparently relations have soured between the two countries, and David exterminates two-thirds of their men, with the rest becoming his slaves. Moab remains subservient to Israel for many years to come.

Zobah is a small Syrian kingdom north of Damascus. Evidently David defeats this tiny but aspiring nation as he marches northward toward the Euphrates. Zobah's defeat prompts retaliation against David from other Syrian groups, such as Damascus, who are promptly conquered and enslaved. David collects considerable booty from these groups. The writer credits the Lord with the successes of all David's exploits (verse 6).

Hamath is a city in the northern part of Syria, above Zobah. When their king, Toi, learns that David has defeated Zobah, he quickly moves to establish peaceful diplomatic relations. He sends his own son, Joram, as his personal envoy, bearing many gifts and friendly greetings. The Lord receives a proper share of these gifts, as is appropriate.

Edom is located south of Moab, east of the Jordan River. The Valley of Salt has not been located exactly, but seems to have been close to the Dead Sea, in a depression east of that site. David establishes military outposts throughout the region, and enslaves most of the suitable population.

The list of David's officials suggests the formal beginnings of a governmental bureaucracy. Joab is his chief military officer, particularly because of his leadership in the conquest of Jerusalem. He heads up David's national army (as distinct from David's private militia). A *recorder* seems to have been a foreign relations minister. Zadok appears here for the first time, and shares priestly responsibilities with Abiathar (not Ahimelech). During Solomon's reign, Zadok is elevated to the highest cultic office, and Abiathar is banished.

The *secretary* is a royal scribe, in charge of public documents. The Cherethites and Pelethites are David's personal bodyguards. Finally, David's sons also served as priests, and completed the royal cabinet. This list is repeated in 2 Samuel 20:23-26 with only slight variations. David's sons are not mentioned in that list.

§ § § § § § §

The Message of 2 Samuel 5–8

Three major issues emerge from a study of 2 Samuel 5–8: (1) The nature of the Davidic covenant, (2) worship in Israel, and (3) the unlimited nature of God's freedom.

The Davidic covenant contains three promises. First, it distinguishes David as one of the great kings of all the earth. Second, it establishes the Israelites in Palestine and gives them rest and peace. Third, it establishes a dynasty for David so that his descendants will rule over the people of God forever. The fulfillment of these promises has made David an important ruler in the history of Israel. For the biblical writer, this covenant serves two purposes. First, it explains why David did not build the Temple. And second, it provides a theological sanction for kingship.

Worship can be a form of celebration. When David and his band of companions retrieve the ark from Kiriath-jearim (Baale-judah), they march toward Jerusalem in a festive procession. Music and dance are interspersed with sacrificial offerings. This activity illustrates the joyous and emotive nature of worship. The people have something to celebrate, and they give full vent to their joy. Worship is, truly, celebration.

God's freedom is unlimited. By refusing to allow David to build a house, God indicates that there are no limits to the divine freedom to move about. For the moment God became institutionalized, God's spontaneity would disappear. The message is that human attempts to limit God will fail.

§ § § § § § §

Introduction to These Chapters

The action in 2 Samuel 9–12 is an interplay between David's personal behavior (his active concern for Mephibosheth and his adultery with Bathsheba) and his military activity against Aram and Ammon. He satisfied his covenant *(hesed)* obligation to Jonathan by honoring and endowing his son, Mephibosheth, with a fealty. In his adulterous relationship with Bathsheba, he exhibits flagrant abuse of his royal power. David pays a very high price for their sin, since its effects continue to trouble him the rest of his days. On another front, David brings his military career to a successful conclusion with battles against Aram and Ammon. Both kingdoms are soundly defeated, and are incorporated within David's large and wealthy empire. But it is David's domestic scene that next forms the arena of turmoil.

Here is an outline of these chapters.

I. David's Concern for Mephibosheth (9:1-13)
II. David Wars Against Ammon and Aram (10:1-19)
III. David's Sin with Bathsheba (11:1–12:31)

David's Concern for Mephibosheth (9:1-13)

Out of a combination of personal affection and covenant loyalty to Jonathan, David seeks out his sole remaining son, Mephibosheth, and shows great concern for him. David brings Mephibosheth to Jerusalem and assigns him all economic benefits from Saul's royal holdings. Ziba, a servant of Saul, is to be the overseer of Mephibosheth's lands, while his master dines regularly at David's table.

This chapter presupposes the horrible events described in 2 Samuel 21:1-14. There, a famine forces David to release Saul's remaining seven sons to the Gibeonites, who promptly hang them in revenge for what Saul did to them. Although the Old Testament makes no mention of any such action, earlier in his reign Saul seems to have executed substantial numbers of this tribe (21:1). Accordingly, a state of bloodguilt existed between the house of Saul and the Gibeonites. In his anger toward Saul, God caused the famine. Expiation required, therefore, that Saul's remaining family be sacrificed—all except Mephibosheth. Thus, in 9:1, it is understandable that David has difficulty in discovering *anyone left of the house of Saul.*

The expression *kindness* (verses 1, 3, and 7) means much more than respect or compassion. The term *hesed* signifies a kind of legal obligation rooted in a strong bond of friendship, such as was characteristic of Jonathan and David. David has sworn to preserve Jonathan's name (1 Samuel 20) and is bound by oath to this obligation, David can also keep a watchful eye on any potential rival to his throne.

An explanation for Mephibosheth's lameness (verses 3 and 13) is provided in 2 Samuel 4:4, which indicates that he accidentally fell while fleeing to safety following events at Mount Gilboa. Even so, his lameness was less than completely debilitating since he sired a son, Mica. As mentioned earlier, the name *Mephibosheth* was changed from *Meri-baal,* to avoid having a royal descendant named after a pagan god. Machir, son of Ammiel, lived at Lodebar, a city in the Transjordan region, possibly close to Mahanaim. Saul apparently retained considerable support in this region as his descendants were able to find refuge in a time of danger.

Mephibosheth's initial fear in David's presence is perhaps well-founded, in view of David's actions to Saul's seven remaining sons (21:1-14). He thinks he might be killed, also. He is astonished to learn of David's intentions to honor him with a place at the royal table, as well as to provide him with a sizable endowment. His comparison to a *dog* (verse 8) is a term of self-abasement. Ziba, Saul's servant, is appointed to tend the royal field, which may have been located well outside Jerusalem, possibly in the Transjordan. But Ziba's family is sufficiently large (15 sons plus 20 servants) for the task. Ziba's designation as a servant does not imply economic servitude, but social class. Ziba later accuses Mephibosheth of treason, but is proven to be lying (19:24-30).

Mephibosheth's son, Mica, preserves Saul's dynasty and satisfies David's obligation to preserve the family of Jonathan.

David Wars Against Ammon and Aram (10:1-19)

Having already conquered the Philistines, Edom, and Moab, and established favorable diplomatic relations with other nations north to the Euphrates, David confronts a strong coalition from Ammon and Syria. With the help of Joab in an initial encounter at Rabbah, David meets the Syrians and registers a stunning victory. A second offensive by the Arameans is no more successful than the first effort. David is now *the* premier leader from Egypt to the Euphrates.

The stimulus for David's attack against the Ammonites is provided by an ungracious and contemptuous act toward Israelite emissaries. Nahash, king of Ammon, has just died. Although this same Nahash earlier had bad relations with King Saul (1 Samuel 11), he and David have apparently established some type of formal, friendly relationship. David is proper in expressing condolences for his ally. But Hanun, Nahash's son, is advised to be cautious, lest these Israelites be spies. So to render them harmless, Hanun publicly humiliates them by shaving off their beards and exposing their genitals. It is little wonder that David exercises great compassion when he learns the unfortunate plight of his emissaries. This insult cannot be ignored, so David prepares for war.

In anticipation of David's attack, the Ammonites hire mercenary soldiers from Syria, and from the nearby states of Maccah and Tob. The two latter regions are located in the Transjordan, north of Ammon. Joab leads a contingent of Israelite troops northward. The first battle seems to center at Rabbah, near the city gate. The Ammonites are positioned just outside the gate as bait, while the mercenaries station themselves a short distance away. The plan is to lure Joab and his army in close to the gate, then attack from the rear. Anticipating this tactic, Joab divides his army and sends in one contingent under Abishai, his brother. Joab challenges the Syrians in the open field. When the Ammonites see Joab winning, they retreat quickly back into the city. Obviously, Joab's tactical judgment is sound.

David's army seems to be structured into three layers. The *host of Israel* or *all of Israel* is the largest unit, and consists of men drafted from all the tribes under David's authority. Usually, Joab is the leader of this group. The second level is known as David's *mighty men*. Basically these are his highly trained militia, many of whom have been with David since his early days in Judah. Abishai is their leader. Finally, the third layer is a select group of men, under Benach, who serve as David's personal bodyguards. The Cherethites and Pelethites are included in this group.

But the Syrians are stubborn adversaries, and regroup for a second engagement against Israel. This time, the two top commanders and even the kings lead their troops, David for Israel and Hadadezer and Shobach (the general) for Syria. As earlier, the Israelites convincingly defeat the Syrians, so that they become Israelite vassals and trouble David no more. Subjugation of the Ammonites must wait until a later time.

David's Sin with Bathsheba (11:1–12:31)

The setting of this story (which, incidentally, is omitted by the Chronicler since it presents David in such a negative light), is Jerusalem in springtime. David's troops are away, doing battle with Ammon, and David has chosen to remain at home. Joab is in charge of the army.

Late in the afternoon, David is strolling atop his roof (roofs were—and still are—flat) when by chance he notices a beautiful woman bathing. He inquires as to her identity, and is told that the woman is Bathsheba, the wife of Uriah the Hittite. She is also identified by her father, Eliam, who appears again in 23:34 as the son of Ahithophel. Uriah is a member of David's select group of soldiers, known as The Thirty (23:13, 39). As will be evident shortly, this non-Israelite displays more faithfulness to God's prohibitions during holy war than does David himself.

David succumbs to lust (presumably) and sends for Bathsheba. As it happened, Bathsheba has just completed her menstrual period and is *purifying* herself. They sleep together, and a child is conceived from this union.

When David learns of Bathsheba's pregnancy, he sends immediately for Uriah in hopes of shifting the burden of paternity onto his shoulders. He cleverly disguises his real motives behind a facade of concern for the war effort. As a reward for his bravery and his service, Uriah is told to go to his house and *wash his feet* (a euphemism for sexual intercourse). But Uriah knows the rules of abstinence during holy war. Furthermore, his conscience prohibits him from relaxing in comfort while his fellow soldiers sleep in the open fields. He refuses to visit

Bathsheba. David's next plan involves intoxication, but even this does not work.

In desperation, David writes Joab a note and has Uriah deliver it. This note details a plan to have Uriah killed in battle. Although the plan does not go exactly as proposed, it is nevertheless successful and Uriah dies in battle (needlessly). Joab sends a messenger to David with the news of battle, concluding with an appendix that Uriah has died, also. Uriah's death resulted from poor military tactics, approaching too close to the city wall. But David's callous response (verse 25, paraphrased, "you win some, you lose some"), excuses Joab's actions since they have achieved the desired results.

With Uriah dead, and a respectable period of mourning observed, David and Bathsheba wed. But this is not the end of the matter, for *the thing that David had done displeased the* LORD. David must accept the responsibility for his sin. Specifically, David is guilty on two accounts: (1) a moral sin—adultery, and (2) accessory to murder.

Nathan's parable (12:1-6) is a poignant and effective means of introducing the Lord's condemnation in verses 7-12. The rich man's theft of the poor man's lamb must have evoked rage and anger in the hearers, and David is no exception. He concludes that the rich man deserves to die and should make restitution *fourfold* (NRSV; NIV, *four times over*). With this indictment, David writes his own condemnation by Nathan's famous words, *You are the man!* Now that David realizes *he* is the rich man who stands convicted, Nathan can deliver the Lord's announcement of judgment.

Through Nathan, the Lord reminds David that his success, his wealth, and even his life, have all been gifts from the Lord. Now David's sin is very grave. He must face the consequences: (1) perennial violence within his immediate family, and (2) personal humiliation by the seduction of his concubines, in full view of all Israel.

Nathan indicates that the Lord has forgiven David's sin (meaning that the Lord will not require David's own life). But Uriah's blood must be atoned for, in this instance, by the death of the illegitimate child (verses 13-14).

The notion that God demands the life of a child as atonement for sin is difficult for modern ears. But we must remember that the Old Testament was written in an age long ago, at a time when religious views differed from those of today. God demanded justice. Uriah's blood had been wrongly shed; now the child must relinquish his life.

To change God's mind, David prostrates himself before the Lord in fasting and prayer (verse 16). He continues this intense mourning for seven days, until he learns that the child is dead. Then, he arises, bathes, and goes to the Temple. Following prayers, he returns home and eats. In explaining his seeming indifference to the child's death, David says that while the child lived, he exerted every possible effort on his behalf. But now that he is dead, there is nothing more he can do for the child.

David and Bathsheba console each other (verse 24), and she gives birth to another son. And they call him Solomon, or perhaps Jedediah (verse 25). Some scholars argue that Jedediah was his personal (birth) name, and Solomon was his throne name. The name Jedediah is not mentioned again.

David's Final Conquest of Ammon (12:26-31)

With these two battles, David completes his conquest of the Ammonites. These neighbors are located almost due east, across the Jordan River from the city of Jericho. They remain servants of Israel until well after Solomon's death in 922 B.C.

Verses 26 and 27 refer to a special section of Rabbah, close to the water supply. By identifying the sector as royal, the writer may imply that it was the location of the king's palace or the administrative center of the Ammonite capital.

Joab properly waits for David before making the final assault against the city. David's authority over Rabbah is shown by the fact that it will be called by Joab's name. While Joab has qualities that characterize him as vicious and dangerous, he is nonetheless intensely loyal and respectful to David. At no time does he infringe on royal prerogative or challenge David's office. Probably, he is David's most avid supporter.

In verse 30, *their king* should be read *Milcom,* referring to the Ammonite deity. In Hebrew, these two words have very similar consonants, and one word could easily have been confused for another. This reference is noted in the Revised Standard Version in a footnote.

The spoils of war taken from Rabbah are many and of great value. The crown alone, taken from the head of their god, Milcom, is worth a fortune. In addition to the great wealth taken from the cities, David enslaves large numbers of the Ammonites, and puts them to work on royal construction crews.

§ § § § § § §

The Message of 2 Samuel 9-12

Two important issues emerge from 2 Samuel 9–12:
(1) David's obligation to God, and (2) the results of sin.
David satisfies his covenant obligations. He brings
Mephibosheth, Jonathan's son, to the royal palace in
Jerusalem, and bestows great honor and kindness upon
him. Jonathan and David had made a covenant (1 Samuel
20:12-17). So David is fulfilling much more than a legal
obligation to Mephibosheth. He is fulfilling his word of
promise sworn to his beloved friend Jonathan.

Sin results in both punishment and forgiveness. David
commits adultery with Bathsheba, and to cover up his
mistake he orders the death of Uriah, her husband. These
actions violate God's commandments, they violate Israelite
morality, and they even violate civil codes. Moreover, these
sins are an abuse of royal power—exactly the sort of thing
Samuel feared (1 Samuel 8:10-18).

David's sin affects several persons—Uriah, the child,
Joab, Nathan, and others. Most of all, the sin angers God.
For that David must be punished.

David's sins must be expiated. One of the more
troublesome issues in this section is the image of a
vengeful God requiring the life of an innocent child. In
early Israel, the concept of expiation involved satisfaction
of obligation to God. When a person sinned against the
Lord, certain means existed to obtain forgiveness.
Particularly in the case of shedding innocent blood, the
blood of the perpetrator was required in return. But
substitutions were permissible, and here the child,
conceived in sin, became an alternative to the king. Thus,
from an ancient perspective, David's sins were atoned
for, fairly, by the life of his son.

§ § § § § § §

2 Samuel 13–16

Introduction to These Chapters

Second Samuel 13–16 contains some of the most morally debased material in the Old Testament. The strife that divides the royal family is created not only by personal rivalries within David's house, but also by divine judgment. This is the fulfillment of Nathan's oracle.

Here is an outline of these chapters.

I. Tamar's Rape (13:1-22)
II. Absalom's Revenge (13:23-38)
III. Absalom's Return (14:1-33)
IV. Absalom's Revolt (15:1-37)
V. Absalom Enters Jerusalem (16:1-23)

Tamar's Rape (13:1-22)

Tamar's status as a virgin daughter of the king made her of exceptionally great value. Often, international diplomacy required marriages of the daughters of kings, and only virgins were suitable mates for other kings. Being of such great worth, Tamar would have been carefully watched. It is little wonder that *it seemed impossible to him to do anything to her* (verse 2).

Jonadab, Amnon's friend, is *shrewd* (NIV; NRSV, *crafty*). The Hebrew term is *hakam,* usually translated as *wise*. Actually, the term *hakam* designates superior intellect without judging the morality of the actions pursued. The meanings of *hakam* range from morally prudent to crafty. Obviously, Jonadab's intentions in the present situation are less than noble. As will become clear later in this story, Jonadab seizes every opportunity to ingratiate himself to persons in power.

Since illness is viewed with great seriousness, Jonadab and Amnon know David will be willing to grant almost any request. Also, David would be especially concerned for the well-being of his eldest son, his heir apparent. If specially prepared food can revive the ailing lad, then David is all for the idea. Perhaps there is a quasi-magical quality about food prepared in sight of the person who is ill.

Tamar's preparations are described. She kneads the dough and bakes (boils) the bread in full view of Amnon. But when she is ready to serve him, he orders the room to be vacated, invites Tamar into the bedroom, and propositions her. Her refusal reflects her own moral misgivings, as well as society's mores. Amnon himself will appear like a *fool* (NIV; NRSV, *scoundrel*)—he will be violating a sexual custom that protects fundamental human dignity. Incest is wrong (Leviticus 18:9). Perhaps, Tamar suggests, David may be willing to suspend the law in this case and allow them to marry. But Tamar's pleading is to no avail. Amnon compounds the sin of incest with the sin of rape.

Suddenly, Amnon's passionate love turns to deep hate, and he orders Tamar out of his chamber. Again, she pleads with him to at least accept responsibility for what he has done, and not doubly compound his sin. Amnon violates another custom or law that requires the man who seduces a virgin to provide payment (Exodus 22:16-17).

Greatly ashamed, Tamar tears her special clothing as a sign of mourning, or possibly to signify her loss of virginity. She symbolizes her shame by placing her hand on her head, and seeks haven with Absalom, her brother. Her value (and self-esteem) have suffered a tragic blow, through no fault of hers. Absalom must guess what has happened (verse 20). Unfortunately, we learn nothing more of Tamar's fate. But Absalom broods for revenge, and quietly awaits a more opportune moment. Unfortunately, David does nothing to punish Amnon.

Absalom's Revenge (13:23-38)

Absalom waits two years before he is able to avenge the rape of Tamar. His motive in waiting two years may be to lull Amnon, and possibly David also, into thinking that the Tamar incident is forgotten. Or perhaps he has not yet had the proper opportunity.

One of the great festivals in a pastoral society was the sheepshearing feast. Since there would be much drinking and revelry, it would be the perfect occasion for an assassination. The site of this great festival is Baal-hazor, some eighteen miles north of Jerusalem. This would be a safe distance away from David's city. Plans are made and set into motion. Absalom can satisfy his thirst for revenge and, at the same time, eliminate a rival claimant for the throne of David.

Absalom extends an invitation to attend to David and to all his servants. But David refuses, suggesting that such a large delegation would create too much of a problem. So Absalom tells David to send Amnon as his proxy. David seems reluctant, but finally agrees to allow Amnon to go. He may be a little suspicious of Absalom's motives, and afraid for Amnon's safety. Meanwhile, Absalom and his servants develop a plot to kill Amnon while he is drunk. The plan works to perfection. Then everyone scatters in panic. Since horses were uncommon in Israel at this time (too expensive), royalty rode mules (18:9) or donkeys (16:1).

A report comes to David that all his sons have been killed. But an opportunistic Jonadab corrects this rumor, arguing that it is only Amnon who has been killed. Jonadab explains that Absalom has been plotting revenge for Tamar's rape for two years, and that now he has satisfied his desire for Amnon's blood. That Jonadab chose to remain in Jerusalem, rather than attend the festival at Baal-hazor, is interesting in itself. Did he suspect foul play? At any rate, his words to David are proven true when the royal mules and their riders are spied.

Meanwhile, Absalom flees into self-imposed exile to the home of his grandfather, Tahmai, king of Geshur. He remains here for three years. As David copes successfully with Amnon's death, he begins to wish for Absalom's return. Is he concerned about Absalom or is he worried about who will succeed him as king?

Absalom's Return (14:1-33)

The phrase *the king's heart longed for Absalom* (NIV; NRSV, *the king's mind was on*) means that David's grief over Amnon was abated to the point that revenge against Absalom no longer haunts his thoughts. Judging from his later treatment of his son, however, David has by no means forgiven Absalom. He is concerned about his son, and about the successor to his throne.

The wise woman of Tekoa is clever and imaginative. Joab intends to use her talents to help David see the need to recall Absalom. Together, Joab and this woman create a guise to entangle David. She invents a story in which one of her two sons kills his brother, following a bitter argument. Now the woman's family is determined to take the life of the remaining son, in blood vengeance for the life of his brother. The woman then will be left with no son to carry on the family name. She pleads with David for special intercession, and the king grants her petition.

Then, the woman requests an additional word with the king, and discloses what is really on her mind. With Absalom in exile, Israel has no clear successor to David, and the people are frightened lest David die and Absalom remain in exile. They fear their enemies will seize the opportunity to attack them. She pleads with

David to allow Absalom to return. Her attempt to resume her fictitious role as a widow fails, and David exposes her plot (verse 19).

The woman tries flattering David twice by comparing his wisdom to the wisdom of God. Without reacting to the deceitful ploy, David sends immediately and brings Absalom home from Geshur. David recognizes the need to set aside all obligations for bloodguilt (even within a family) for the sake of community interest.

Verses 25-27 interrupt the narrative to furnish a brief description of Absalom's physical appearance, particularly his hair. Like his father, Absalom is a strikingly attractive man. Also like David, Absalom marries a beautiful woman. Their daughter bears the same name as Absalom's sister, Tamar. Further, Absalom attracts a popular following. These similarities are not coincidental.

David punishes Absalom further by refusing to meet with him for two years. David's chief difficulty as a parent with Amnon was leniency; now with Absalom his problem is severity. His motives in ignoring Absalom are anger, fear, and ignorance. Even Joab refuses to speak with Absalom until Absalom's servant sets fire to Joab's field. Joab then speaks with David and David receives Absalom. The kiss (verse 33) indicates forgiveness and acceptance.

But Absalom will long remember how David ignored him, and the resentment will combine with eagerness for David's throne to spark a rebellion. David does not handle this matter with his earlier military expertise. He lacks the good judgment as a father that he possessed as a military leader.

Absalom's Revolt (15:1-37)

Several years pass following David's reconciliation with Absalom. During this time, Absalom begins to brood over David's earlier treatment (14:28). Since the procedure for determining succession has not yet been established, Absalom becomes concerned that he be denied David's royal office. Thus he decides to take matters into his own hands to ensure his future as Israel's king. To convey a public image of royalty, Absalom parades throughout the land in a chariot, accompanied by runners, in the tradition of ancient Near Eastern monarchs. Also, he sows seeds of dissatisfaction among those who come to Jerusalem seeking an audience with David. Absalom feigns a personal interest in their case, and suggests better treatment for them if only he were king. He flatters them further with a royal kiss. With these actions, Absalom begins to attract a sizable following who will support him in his revolt. His physical attractiveness and winsome personality make Absalom very popular.

Absalom prepares to make his move, under the foil of a trip to Hebron, David's first capital, to worship the Lord. David senses no sinister motives in Absalom's request. Absalom's reasons for selecting Hebron as the site of his revolt are not explained. Possibly he chose this city precisely because it would not have evoked suspicion, being David's first capital. Also, it was the site of his birth. Hebron was an important political center in the south, where Absalom might gain additional support.

Ahithophel, Bathsheba's grandfather, accompanies him, along with 200 other persons who have no idea of Absalom's planned revolt. The 200 persons now find themselves in an impossible situation. If they try to return to Jerusalem, Absalom will kill them; if they stay, David will consider them traitors. As plans are finalized for the actual coup, more and more people join the conspiracy. Many persons still blame David for duplicity in the death of Saul and his family. Clearly, David has made a few enemies on his march to the throne; now these malcontents have a leader.

Meanwhile, word reaches David that many persons

have defected to Absalom. Knowing full well that Absalom intends to stage a rebellion, David assembles his family, his personal army, and a few trusted advisors, and begins a march out of Jerusalem. It is a complete mystery as to why the king would flee such a strong and well-fortified city as Jerusalem. Surely he could have resisted an attack by Absalom.

Along the way, several persons show up who wish to accompany David, including Ittai the Gittite. But David urges him to return, since he has been in David's camp only a few days, and David has no idea where he is going at the moment. But Ittai's loyalty is unshakable, and he joins the procession. The Gittites are from Gath, and this episode illustrates David's continued appeal to certain segments of the Philistines.

The brook of Kidron (verse 23) flows along a deep valley that separates Jerusalem from the Mount of Olives on the east. As they pause here, or at the outskirts of Jerusalem, Abiathar and Zadok appear bearing the ark of the covenant. But David sends them back, explaining that God will prevail, with or without the ark. Moreover, he needs them and their sons, Ahimaaz and Jonathan, as spies.

As David processes he prays that the Lord will turn the counsel of Ahithophel into foolishness. At the top of the hill, he is approached by Hushai, his *friend*. Here, the word *friend* designates an office in the government (1 Kings 4:5), possibly like that of an advisor. But Hushai is told that he will be too much of a liability (perhaps due to his age), and his services could be of more value in Jerusalem where he could keep an eye on Absalom. As matters develop, Hushai plays an important role in providing Absalom bad advice.

Absalom Enters Jerusalem (16:1-23)

The first incident in this chapter is Ziba's appearance, bearing provisions and donkeys for David. Clearly, his motives are to curry the favor of the king, in case he survives this latest challenge. When asked about Mephibosheth, Ziba claims that his master wants to reclaim Saul's empire. This claim later turns out to be completely false (19:27-29). But in his haste, David assigns Mephibosheth's possessions to Ziba.

The next scene occurs at Bahurim, a few miles south of the site of the Ziba incident. David is heading for Mahanaim, across the Jordan. Suddenly, he is beset by an angry Shimei, cursing the king and hurling dust from across a narrow ravine. Apparently, Shimei holds David responsible for the disaster that fell upon Saul's house. More specifically, by calling David a *man of blood* (verse 7), he links David either to the deaths of Abner and Ishbosheth or even to the deaths of Saul and Jonathan—or possibly to all four deaths. David responds not in anger, but in stoic acceptance that Shimei's curse is divinely motivated. This may be God's judgment, says David. Perhaps, once this judgment has passed, the Lord may act graciously. Finally, David's party reaches the Jordan River and pauses to rest and to await news of events in Jerusalem.

Back in Jerusalem, Absalom and his contingent of rebels have entered the city and assumed control. Almost immediately, Hushai, David's friend, presents himself to Absalom, and declares his loyalty. Absalom interrogates Hushai as to how he could change loyalties so quickly. But Hushai completely fools Absalom by citing his aquiescence to divine will as well as popular enthusiasm for the new king. With a curious irony, Hushai pledges the same support to Absalom that he gave to his father—loyalty. Hushai's award-winning performance will be of immense benefit later in the story.

Demonstrating his wisdom, Ahithophel urges Absalom to declare his sovereignty over David's empire by taking over his concubines. This is a traditional act of authority, enacted by an incoming king. Absalom wastes no time in conforming to Ahithophel's counsel, just as Nathan had announced earlier (12:11-12). Absalom's rebellion was now irreversible.

§ § § § § § §

The Message of 2 Samuel 1–16

Two important issues emerge from 2 Samuel 13–16: (1) The nature of David's faith in God, and (2) the fulfillment of prophecy.

Faith in the Lord differs from faith in human counsel. When David orders Abiathar and Zadok to return the ark to Jerusalem, he prepares himself to accept God's will. This kind of trust has characterized all of David's early career, when he consulted the Lord prior to nearly every venture. Yet, at the time David is submissive to God's leadership, he actively does all within his power to act prudently. This is faith as active submission.

By contrast, Absalom relies on his own emotions and on the wise counsel of others, never once on God. He is a perfect contrast with his father. The object of his trust leads him to death.

Nathan's prophecy is fulfilled. Nathan's oracle announced that David's house would be continually ravaged by the sword, and that a member of his own house would have intercourse with his concubines, in full view of all Jerusalem. Both these announcements came to pass exactly as described. The biblical writer believes firmly that what God declared through the mouth of Nathan the prophet has come to pass in David's household.

§ § § § § § §

2 Samuel 17–20

Introduction to These Chapters

In 2 Samuel 17–20, David's struggle with Absalom comes to a tragic climax with the battle in the Ephraim forest. Most scholars regard this section as being of considerable historical value. The intimate details of David's moods, Absalom's faulty decisions, and the stern reprimands of Joab all suggest a source very close to the events themselves.

Here is an outline of 2 Samuel 17–20.
   I. Ahithophel's Counsel Rejected (17:1-23)
  II. Absalom's Death (17:24–19:8a)
 III. David's Return to Jerusalem (19:8b-43)
  IV. Sheba's Rebellion (20:1-26)

Ahithophel's Counsel Rejected (17:1-23)

Chronologically, events in chapters 17–20 follow almost immediately after Absalom's entry into Jerusalem and his seizure of David's concubines (16:22). Ahithophel's proposal to launch an immediate attack against David has real merit. First, David must rely on his smaller force, consisting of the mercenaries and a few hundred *mighty men.* Second, they have just stopped after a lengthy march, and they will be tired and somewhat disorganized. The presence of women and children has slowed the march considerably. Third, they will not expect a quick attack at this moment. Finally, an initial blow will panic David's troops. So all the odds are in Ahithopel's favor. As an extra incentive, Ahithophel promises to kill David alone, and bring the rest of his entourage back (verse 3). Clearly, Absalom and his advisors are attracted to Ahithophel's proposal. But they delay in order to solicit an opinion from Hushai. David's friend makes the most of the opportunity offered to him. He suggests an alternative plan, and carefully (subtly) points to weaknesses in Ahithophel's plan. First, he says, David will be even more ferocious than usual, like a bear *robbed of her cubs* (verse 8). Second, David, as a seasoned soldier, will not camp in the grass field inviting attack. He will be difficult to find. Third, the first noise of battle will more likely spook Absalom's troops than David's veterans. So, Hushai argues, Absalom should wait until a large, overpowering army can be assembled and destroy David by force of numbers. Hushai's promise of a glorious and all-out victory are more temptation than Absalom can stand.

Absalom and his advisors find Hushai's plan even more attractive than Ahithophel's proposal, so they agree to wait. God has now heeded David's prayer to frustrate the counsel of Ahithophel (15:31). The writer makes certain his readers recognize that Hushai's success (and Ahithophel's failure) are the result of divine intervention. The Lord allows for David's punishment but does not sanction his death or total destruction.

Once Absalom's decision is made, a prearranged communications network kicks into motion. Hushai notifies Abiathar and Zadok, David's priests. They, in turn, send a young woman to Enrogel (just outside Jerusalem's northeast section). Actually, the plan of communication is rather clever. The woman used as a messenger would be perceived as going to fetch water. Jonathan and Ahimaaz would not bring undue attention to their fathers. She delivers the message to Jonathan and Ahimaaz, sons of Abiathar and Zadok. Unfortunately they are seen, and flee to Bahurim where they are hidden in a well by persons loyal to David. As soon as they can, they hurry to David with the message to cross the Jordan immediately. The reason for the urgency is not clear; perhaps Hushai thought (incorrectly) that Ahithophel's plan had been accepted, thus endangering David's life. Or perhaps Hushai thought David needed to move on before stopping. At any rate, David heeds the message and crosses the Jordan. Meanwhile, Absalom and his army remain in Jerusalem to add numbers to their size.

Realizing that Absalom has made a fatal misjudgment, Ahithophel sets his affairs in order, and hangs himself. He must have realized that once David reorganized, Absalom had no chance of victory. Rather than face a trial for treason, Ahithophel executes himself. Since there are so few suicides in the Old Testament, we may deduce that such a practice was viewed negatively.

Absalom's Death (17:24–19:8a)

Following a brief notice that Ahithophel ended his own life (17:23), the narrator resumes his account of David's escape. Having crossed the Jordan, David finds safety at Mahanaim. Mahanaim is an odd place for David to seek refuge and to reorganize for a counterattack against Absalom and the troops of Israel. This is the city to which Ishbosheth and Abner fled following the defeat of Saul's army at Mount Gilboa. It is located well across the Jordan River, in the region known as the Transjordan.

Absalom's appointment of Amasa, a relative of Joab, suggests that deep factionalism existed within the royal family. Amasa is related in some way to Joab; possibly they are cousins. Later, David appoints Amasa to a major post within his new government back in Jerusalem to strengthen his ties to Judah.

The Abigail mentioned in 17:25 is obviously not the same Abigail who married David. Neither is Nahash the king of the Ammonites with whom David had established friendly relations. *Ithra* (NRSV) is called *Jether* (NIV) in 1 Kings 2:5, 32 and 1 Chronicles 2:17.

Some members of the diplomatic entourage who visit David support the king probably not because of any particular affection or loyalty, but out of a blend of fear and respect. Once David regains his throne (and no one, except possibly Absalom, doubts that he will regain it) he can inflict considerable pain upon anyone of questionable loyalty. As for Machir and Barzillai, he deserves their complete support since he has had nothing to do with the destruction of the house of Saul.

David reorganizes his army into three parts: one under Joab, another under Abishai, and a third under Ittai. Although he readies himself for battle, his men urge him to remain at Mahanaim, in safety. David's value is incalculable. The well-being of the nation is thought to be connected to the well-being of the king. An injury to the king, or worse, his death, would spell doom for the nation. He agrees to remain at home, but admonishes them, in the hearing of everyone present, to protect Absalom.

The forest of Ephraim (verse 6) is located somewhere in the Transjordan area, south of the Jabbok River. According to the text, the area is hilly, densely forested, and intently foreboding. David could not have chosen a better site to neutralize Absalom's numerically superior army. His plan works well, and Absalom's troops scatter in complete disarray. Some are killed outright, while others the forest devoured (verse 8).

Confusion and ignomy surround the death of Absalom. While trying to escape, Absalom's mule (the common mount of royalty) carries his rider beneath a tree with low branches. Absalom's head becomes caught in a fork, jerking Absalom instantly from his mount and leaving him dangling helplessly in midair. Joab hurls three darts (or spears) into the rebellious lad. Whether Absalom dies as a consequence of Joab's darts (or spears) is unclear. Removing responsibility for his death from Joab, ten armor bearers finish the job. Now the revolt is really over. Joab clearly cares more for the security and welfare of the nation than for David's personal feelings. Absalom is thrown into a nameless pit and covered with rocks. He is not extended the courtesy of burial in the monument he had previously built for himself.

Joab sends the news of the victory to David by way of a Cushite (Ethiopian) messenger, only after denying an enthusiastic Ahimaaz (son of Zadok). Either Ahimaaz does not yet know Absalom is dead (and Joab prefers to withhold that information at the moment), or else Joab senses that Ahimaaz is too intimately involved with David to present Absalom's death in the proper context. So the Cushite sets out to tell David. But Ahimaaz refuses to give up and continues to plead with Joab, until Joab finally gives in. Ahimaaz speeds away, takes a better road to Mahanaim, and arrives ahead of the Cushite. He informs the king that the battle has gone well, but David cares more about the welfare of Absalom. When asked the same question, the Cushite politely invokes a fate similar to Absalom's upon all the enemies of David (verse 32). But David gets the point that Absalom is dead.

David responds to the news as a father, not as a king. When Joab learns of David's reaction, he goes immediately to David and points out that instead of thanking the soldiers and the people for their support and their courage, he has shamed them into guilt by his preoccupation with Absalom. David recognizes the truth of Joab's argument, sets aside his paternal feelings, and goes to welcome his returning troops and supporters.

David's Return to Jerusalem (19:8b-43)

With Absalom dead and David away in exile in a foreign land, the citizenry of Israel find themselves leaderless. The northern tribes move first to restore David to power. But David insists that his restoration meet with universal approval, including Judah where Absalom's revolt began. After all, these persons are

David's own family! To assure them that full pardons are in order, and that he plans no retaliations, he names Amasa, Absalom's general, as the new commander of the army. Not only is this move good conciliatory politics, but it also constitutes a stern reprimand for Joab's viciousness in the deaths of Abner and Absalom. Judah responds by coming to Gilgal, an important religious site in early Israel, to welcome David home.

As David and his royal party near the west bank of the Jordan, they are met by several persons who played roles in David's departure from Jerusalem earlier. Ziba, Mephibosheth's servant, appears along with his fifteen sons, and transports the king across the river. Shimei, who earlier cursed David as a murderer (16:5-13), comes apologizing and pleading for his life. David is anxious to mend fences and strengthen his ties to the northern tribes, so he extends a full pardon to Shimei.

Mephibosheth appears and explains to David that Ziba lied and that he had indeed wanted to join David as he left Jerusalem. David is seemingly unable to determine which one is telling the truth, so he divides Mephibosheth's inheritance with Ziba.

As David leaves Mehanaim on his return trip to Jerusalem, he is accompanied as far as the Jordan by Barzillai, the aged Gileadite. This wealthy patron had supported David during his brief stay in exile. Now, as David prepares to resume power, the king extends his gratitude to his benefactor. But Barzillai politely declines David's offer because of his age and his desire to be at home as he approaches death. Instead he sends Chimham, his servant, to receive David's favor.

The concluding verses of this chapter (41–43) describe a problem developing between the tribes of Israel and the tribes of Judah. The Israelites appeal to David that they were the first to welcome David back from exile. Why, then, does he favor Judah? This rift grows wider and wider during Solomon's reign. It eventually ruptures under Rehoboam in 925 B.C. with the division into two separate nations—Israel (north) and Judah (south).

Sheba's Rebellion (20:1-26)

The indentification of Sheba as coming from Benjamin attests further to the hostility this tribe harbors toward David. Although Sheba apparently draws support only from his own tribe, the Bichrites, David realizes the potential threat such an uprising can have for his fragile coalition. He wastes no time in moving to counter Sheba's decisive actions. By contrast, the men of Judah loyally follow David to Jerusalem (20:2).

Interrupting the account of this revolt is a brief notice regarding the fate of the ten concubines David had left in charge of the palace when he fled the city. These women were claimed by Absalom (16:22) when he entered Jerusalem. But although this action made them unclean, David graciously sees that they have a home.

David places Amasa in charge of the troops from Judah, but he is less than prompt in executing his duties. To quell Sheba's revolt, David turns to Abishai, Joab's brother. David may still harbor resentment against Joab, or else he is too proud to reassign Joab as commander. At any rate, Joab quickly resolves David's dilemma by brutally killing Amasa, who by this time has joined David's army at Gibeon. Joab is David's most loyal supporter, but he is also the most vicious soldier in David's army.

Joab and Abishai pursue Sheba unnoticed to the very edge of Israelite territory, to the city of Abel Beth-maacah. As Joab's assault against the city gains momentum, a *wise woman* appeals to Joab to spare the city. Joab agrees to call off his assault in exchange for Sheba's head. The woman agrees, and Sheba's life is sacrificed to save the city. The revolt ends almost as quickly as it began.

The list of David's officials in 20:23-26 is similar to the earlier list in 8:1b-18. Here, Sheba is identified as secretary, instead of Seraiah.

§ § § § § § §

The Message of 2 Samuel 17–20

God is active in history, responding to sincere prayers. Just as David flees Jerusalem in the wake of Absalom's revolt, he learns that Ahithophel, one of his advisors, has joined the rebellion. David prays that the Lord turn his counsel into disaster (15:31). In 17:14, God answers David's prayer. Absalom chooses to follow Hushai's advice to delay attacking David rather than heed the proposal of Ahithophel to continue pursuit immediately.

The writer makes the point that this delay was not the result of human calculation. From a theological perspective, Absalom's revolt may be considered a part of God's judgment against David for the Bathsheba affair. Therefore, the revolt is a necessary component in God's plan. But yet, because of David's great faith, the Lord does not intend to allow David to die or his dynasty to fall into the wrong hands. So Absalom's rebellion is doomed to failure, even from the outset. God controls the direction of history.

David's love for Absalom is unconditional. When David learns of Absalom's death, he weeps uncontrollably. This reaction shows a father's sincere and unconditional love for his son. Absalom had done little to earn David's love. His cruel revenge against his brother Amnon, his devious undermining of his father's judicial system, his impatience for power, and finally his revolt all display contempt rather than love. And yet, David loved him deeply. David's love for Absalom was unconditional. Perhaps this same kind of love is reflected in John 3:16, and in God's love for us.

§ § § § § § §

2 Samuel 21–24

Introduction to These Chapters

The final four chapters in 2 Samuel form an appendix
to David's long and successful reign. These chapters
consist of several different literary types: hymns, lists,
hero legends, and historical narratives.

Here is an outline of these chapters.

I. A Famine and David's Response (21:1-14)
II. War with the Philistines (21:15-22)
III. David's Hymn of Praise (22:1-51)
IV. David's Second Song (23:1-7)
V. David's Warriors (23:8-39)
VI. A Census, a Plague, and an Altar (24:1-25)

A Famine and David's Response (21:1-14)

For three years, a severe famine has gripped the nation
of Israel. David consults the Lord, and discovers that the
famine is a result of God's anger toward Saul for
breaking a treaty with the Gibeonites. The Gibeonites
occupied a region three or four miles north of Jerusalem.
They were Canaanites who had managed to trick Joshua
into signing a treaty, exempting them from destruction
(Joshua 9). The Old Testament does not mention a
general massacre of these persons by Saul. God's oracle
(verse 1) must refer to an event not preserved by biblical
historians. Possibly Saul's attack on the Gibeonites was
motivated by his efforts to purge his country of all ethnic
and religious elements alien to Yahweh (1 Samuel 13–15).

David allows the Gibeonites to determine their own form of expiation for Saul's bloodguilt, and thus he remains above bloodshed and violence.

David is able to locate only two of Saul's family members: two sons of Saul (Armoni and Mephibosheth) and his concubine Rizpah. This Mephibosheth is clearly not the son of Jonathan to whom David later extends kindness. The remaining victims are Saul's grandsons, the sons of Merab (identified as Michal in some manuscripts).

The Barzillai mentioned in 21:8 is not the same Barzillai who befriended David at Mahanaim (17:27). The writer reminds us that David spared Mephibosheth, the son of Jonathan, so we can easily understand why David has trouble finding anyone left of Saul's house (assuming that chapter 21 precedes chapter 9), other than Mephibosheth.

The seven victims are hanged atop a neighboring holy mountain, possibly as part of some type of cultic ceremony. Since the men are to serve as an expiation for bloodguilt, their deaths are perceived religiously. The phrase *before the* LORD (verse 9) refers to the notion that God is ceremonially present at the execution.

Rizpah's vigil is a true act of motherly love and devotion. She encamps beside the seven corpses for a very long time to protect them from birds and beasts. Exactly how long her vigil lasts is uncertain—possibly during the entire summer until the fall rains come. Her loyalty evokes David's sense of compassion, and he removes the bodies and provides a proper burial, along with the remains of Saul and Jonathan. The famine ends, and peace returns to Israel because of David's wisdom and faith.

War with the Philistines (21:15-22)

These verses describe conflict with Philistines, and belong chronologically with 5:17-25. Logically, prior to

David's efforts to bring foreign nations into his empire, he must secure internal matters first. In one of these encounters David almost loses his life due to battle fatigue, but is saved by Abishai. His troops beg him to cease his active participation in battle, since the welfare of the nation is tied intimately to the well-being of the king.

The phrase *lamp of Israel* symbolizes the continuing power of the nation. Perhaps this lamp may be understood as analogous to the priestly lamp that burned constantly beside the ark at Shiloh (1 Samuel 3:3). This perception of king and country is also reflected earlier when his troops convince him to remain at Mahanaim rather than pursue Absalom. After all, he is worth *ten thousand* of them (18:3).

Verses 18-22 summarize a series of four encounters by David's men with giants, or Philistine warriors from Gath. The narrator reemphasizes David's enormous power, both physically and personally. The heroic legends add to David's stature as a warrior of both skill and bravery. Gob (verses 18-19) is a site not presently identified.

In verse 19, a certain Elhanan is said to have killed Goliath. Earlier this feat was credited to David (1 Samuel 17:4). Perhaps David and Elhanan are actually the same person, with David being merely a throne name. Or there may have been two Goliaths. Or as 1 Chronicles 20:5 states, Elhanan slew Goliath's brother, Lahmi. Or perhaps David killed a large man who was nameless at first, and who later received the name Goliath. Or perhaps David's fame and legendary status attracted incidents otherwise performed by other individuals.

David's Hymn of Praise (22:1-51)

In the Old Testament we frequently find hymns of praise and thanksgiving at major junctures in Israel's history: the birth of Samuel (1 Samuel 2:1-10); Saul's and

Jonathan's deaths (2 Samuel 1:19-27). At the close of David's career, it is appropriate to find a majestic hymn celebrating God's miraculous deliverance and exaltation of David. This psalm has an almost identical parallel in Psalm 18. Many scholars argue that the present version in 2 Samuel 22 represents a combination of two originally independent hymns that have been joined together. Whether David actually composed this psalm, either as a whole or in part, is equally a matter of disagreement.

The opening verses (2-6) describe the life-threatening plight of David, who calls upon the Lord for deliverance. The epithets used to describe God stem mostly from nature: *rock, horn, stronghold, refuge, fortress*. These terms also convey notions of military power. The imagery suggests that the psalmist is about to drown in the primeval waters of chaos that separate earth from Sheol.

In Hebrew poetry, the standard form is a two-line stich, whose members have a conceptual (rather than a rhyming) pattern. Notice that in verse 7, the first line is a cry to God for help. This same call is made again in the second line. This pattern, where the second line repeats the idea in the first line, is called *synonymous parallelism*. When the second line adds a new thought to the first line, the unit reflects *synthetic parallelism* (verse 18). If the second line presents an idea that is opposite to the idea in the first line, we have *antithetical parallelism* (verse 28).

Verse 7 is David's cry of help. Synonymous parallelism emphasizes his plea and stresses God as the object of his petitions. Lines 3 and 4 of verse 7 emphasize that God has heard his prayer. The petition is simple and direct; the psalmist is confident in the Lord's willingness to provide help after recognizing the psalmist's plight.

Verses 8-16 describe a theophany, a manifestation of God. God now responds to David's plea. Like many theophanies in the Old Testament, God comes through violent outbreaks of earthquakes (verse 8), lightning (verses 9, 15), and fire (verse 13). God rides on a mythical cherub (a winged lion with a human head). The earth bares her soul (verse 16) to the appearance of the Lord. Yet, the Lord is veiled in a *canopy of darkness* (verse 12).

Verses 17-25 describe the Lord's deliverance of the psalmist from nameless but threatening enemies. He continues his metaphor of nearly drowning in primeval waters, and describes his miraculous rescue, landing him safely on a wide and dry land. The exact nature of the deliverance is not told. Rather, the psalmist uses literary and imaginative imagery to convey the unmistakable hand of God. This is more a confession of faith than an eyewitness report of a real-life experience.

Verses 21-25 justify God's rescue in the righteousness and integrity of the psalmist—he deserved to be rescued! David has remained faithful to God, avoiding evil and acting blamelessly. The Lord is a just God, who clearly rewards faithfulness with deliverance.

Verses 26-31 recount God's deliverance, first of the righteous in general, and then of David in particular. The reference to the Lord as David's *lamp* parallels the allusion to David as the *lamp of Israel* in 21:17.

Verses 32-49 describe the loyalty and support the Lord gave David. His military success clearly belongs to the Lord. His diplomatic success (verse 44) came from the Lord. David's political leadership became known far and wide, for the Lord stood behind his faithful servant.

The psalm of thanksgiving concludes with the psalmist's pledge to continue to sing God's praises forever, for the Lord has shown faithfulness and loyalty to David and to his descendants. Obviously, this conclusion is a later addition, since it refers to David in the third person. The confidence and assurances expressed in verses 50-51 are based on what the Lord did for David. And the writer assumes that what the Lord did for David will be done for other persons also. David's hymn of thanksgiving can become our song of thanksgiving as well.

David's Second Song (23:1-7)

Appropriately, David's final words (next to pronouncing Solomon as king in 1 Kings 2:1-9) are a hymn. David's career as Israel's king was born of a divine blessing, so it is fitting for him to conclude his rule with a stirring acknowledgment of his special relationship to God. And it is precisely this relationship that accounts for David's success.

As in the preceding psalm (chapter 22), retribution is the central theological concept. David reasserts God's decision to bless his descendants with an everlasting covenant. The hymn ends with a word of warning to the godless; their fate is to be consumed by fire (verse 7).

The introduction (verse 1) identifies the speaker as David. Then, using synonymous parallelism, David's exalted status is described: (1) his family status as the son of Jesse, (2) his status as God's chosen and esteemed servant, (3) his charismatic endowment as his status of power and authority, and (4) his status as a psalmist. These descriptions cover the entire range of David's experience from his entry into Saul's court until the present time. To be able to telescope such a broad and expansive career into a few verses shows the genius of Hebrew poetry.

Verse 2 is a transitional element that moves from the introduction to the body of the hymn. The important element in this section is the reference to David's receipt of God's Spirit. Not only has this charismatic endowment enabled David to bring honor and international prominence to Israel, but it now allows David to speak in God's name—to function as a prophet. This designation as divine spokesman lends additional weight to David's status. His words now serve as a source of revelation; they are equal to God's words.

The heart of the hymn is an extended simile, comparing the just and faithful rule of a king to natural elements such as the morning sunlight. Both light and rain are necessary elements for successful agriculture; their absence spells almost certain failure. Similarly, the just and faithful rule of a king brings peace and prosperity to a nation. Israel is great precisely because of David, not vice versa.

Verse 5 affirms that David's reign has been perceived by God as being faithful and just. Accordingly, God has rewarded David's house by making an eternal covenant and insuring that David meets success in all his ventures. Through David and his descendants, God shall bless Israel, the chosen people.

The hymn concludes with a declaration that the godless are like thorns, that is, useless. Actually, translation of the Hebrew text is next to impossible. However, the point seems to be that unlike a just and faithful king who brings blessings to a nation, the godless bring violent destruction and disgrace to a nation. Their fate, and that of their followers, is to be consumed by fire.

David's Warriors (23:8-39)

This section is an appendix with three sections. Verses 8-12 describe three of David's heroes who held special positions in the king's military. *The Three* were Josheb-basshebeth, Eleazar, and Shammah, according to this list. For a variant of Josheb-basshebeths name, see 1 Chronicles 11:11 where he is called *Jashobeam*. Each of these men performed heroic acts for David, and distinguished himself by great feats of courage.

Verses 13-17 describe an episode at Adullam, where David was encamped following his recent escape from Saul. The story belongs to an earlier stage of David's career than its present location here would indicate. The writer places it here because it involves three of David's *thirty chief men* (verse 24). Exactly which three men are involved is not said. Apparently, these three soldiers overhear David longing for water from Bethlehem. They slip past the Philistine sentries and boldly go to Bethlehem to fetch David a jug of water. But David is so conscience-stricken that he is unable to drink the water. Since this water could have cost human lives, it became as blood, and had to be ceremonially emptied upon the ground. David's actions here should not be deemed ungracious. In realizing the dangerous risk his thirst caused, he could only return the water to the Lord in an act of contrition. The water was no longer suitable for human consumption. Such an action on David's part certainly must have endeared him to his men. He was genuinely concerned for their well-being.

Verses 18-23 describe the feats of Abishai and Benaiah, both of whom have been mentioned earlier. Abishai is the brother of Joab and served David well, particularly when Joab brought on David's wrath. Benaiah is the commander of the Cherethites and Pelethites, David's personal bodyguards. Despite the gallant and heroic actions of these two soldiers, they did not achieve membership in the three. Requirements for entry into this select circle must have entailed more than heroism.

The final section (24-39) lists the members of the prestigious *Thirty*. This select group were among David's most trusted and capable soldiers, and formed the nucleus of his personal army. Some of these men came from cities in Israel, some came from cities in Judah, and others came from foreign countries. The term *thirty* probably referred to the popular name of the group rather than designating numerical limits.

A Census, a Plague, and an Altar (24:1-25)

Again (verse 1) relates this chapter back to events narrated in 21:1-14, where God's anger results in natural disasters. Ancient Israel had no concept of secondary causes; the Lord was the ultimate cause for all events of nature, both good and bad. When a natural calamity occurred, people automatically concluded that the Lord must be angry, so steps must be taken to make atonement at once.

Verse 1 states that God causes David to instigate a census. Clearly, the census, which most certainly will bring punishment, is the Lord's idea, not David's. Yet David receives the blame and experiences the guilt (24:16). Why the Lord would do this must be understood in relationship to the final section where the Temple site is chosen. God truly moves in mysterious ways. In fact, it is such a theological problem that the author of 1 Chronicles 21:1, who is telling the same story, changes *he* (meaning the Lord) to *Satan* to remove responsibility from God. Evidently the Chronicler failed to see the census as part of God's total plan.

Recognizing the danger in taking the census, Joab protests to David. But David disregards Joab's advice and proceeds with the census. They begin in the Transjordan, at Aroer, and work northward through Gilead, up beyond Dan across to Tyre, then down the coast the length of the country to Beersheba. Basically, they circle the perimeter of the country. According to the text, the census requires nine months and twenty days. They count 1,300,000 fighting men—an unusually high number for such a relatively small territory.

In the Old Testament, a census usually evoked God's wrath. Perhaps a census was viewed as an infringement of God's freedom since it was for military enlistment, or taxation, or both. Possibly, it infringed on some type of religious rite. But even Joab knows the popular superstition regarding a census: It means divine judgment. But he cannot dissuade David from his course of action.

David's conscience begins troubling him upon completion of the census, and he prays for forgiveness, evidently throughout most of the night. The next morning, God speaks to David through Gad, the prophet (see also 1 Samuel 22:5). The Lord gives David three choices, all with multiples of three: (1) a famine for three years, (2) turbulent warfare for three months, or (3) a plague for three days. David's response avoids selecting the second alternative and leaves the matter of choosing one or three up to the Lord. The Lord sends the plague. David prefers God's judgment and the possibility of mercy to warfare.

For one full day the plague ravages Israel. Seventy thousand men die, *from David to Beersheba*, that is, throughout the country. Just as the plague is about to enter Jerusalem, the Lord says "Enough!" The emissary of the Lord, the carrier of the plague, is described as an angel. David pleads with the Lord to hold only him accountable, and to release the people, *sheep*, from the grip of this angel. Possibly David's intercession preceded God's action in verse 16.

Gad appears once again to David and instructs him to go to the thrashing floor of Araunah, the Jebusite, where the plague ended. David does so, and Araunah greets the king in humility and with honor. When he learns the purpose of David's visit, he offers immediately to furnish the site along with all the sacrificial hosts free of charge. David graciously declines Araunah's offer and indicates that true religion is costly and does not come free. So David purchases the site and constructs a new altar for the Lord. This site is to become the location of Solomon's Temple.

§ § § § § § §

The Message of 2 Samuel 21–24

The first theme in 2 Samuel 21–24 concerns the relationship between God and the laws of nature. In 2 Samuel 21:1-14, the writer describes a severe and lengthy famine that afflicts israel because Saul had violated an early agreement with the Gibeonites by murdering many of their number. In order to atone for Saul's bloodguilt, David turns over to the Gibeonites two of Saul's sons and five of his grandsons. Similarly, in chapter 24, God sends an angel with a terrible pestilence as punishment for David's census. Both stories reflect ancient Israel's belief that God controls the immediate cause. All aspects of the natural order are subject to God's will. On the other hand, our modern scientific perspective explains such events differently. In reading the biblical material, we must learn to withhold judgments about nonscientific descriptions of natural events.

The second major theological issue is the merging of religious faith and political leadership. Throughout the accounts of David's reign, the biblical writer has emphasized David's faith. He always consults the Lord before engaging in battle. He provides a haven of safety for Abiathar, the refugee priest from Nob. He refrains from personal violence against Saul and other adversaries. And even when he sins, he is quick to repent and to seek God's forgiveness. From the perspective of the biblical writer, these qualities of faith prompt God to reward David by granting him and his descendants success as military/political leaders. In the person of the king, religious faith and political leadership must come together in synthesis.

§ § § § § § §

Glossary of Terms

Abel-Beth-Maacah: Well-known for its judicial standards. Sheba fled here after his unsuccessful revolt against David.

Abiathar: The priestly son of Ahimelech who escaped the massacre at Nob, and later served David as a priest.

Abigail: The wife first of Nabal, then later of David.

Abijah: The youngest son of Samuel; judge at Beersheba.

Abinadab: The father of Eleazar, Ahio, and Uzzah, the three men associated with the ark David brought to Jerusalem.

Abishai: The brother of Joab and Asahel. Along with Joab, he was the leader of David's army on several occasions.

Abner: The major commander of Saul's army. When Saul died, he, along with Saul's son, formed a government in exile.

Absalom: Son of David and Maacah. His revolt drove David from Jerusalem but ultimately failed and cost him his life.

Achish: Philistine king to whom David fled to avoid Saul.

Adullam: The mountain fortress in Judah to which David fled to escape Saul.

Ahimaaz: (1) The father of Ahinoam, wife of Saul; and (2) the son of Zadok, who carried news of Absalom's death to David.

Ahimelech: The priest at Nob who supplied David with food and a weapon. This service later cost Ahimelech his life.

Ahinoam: (1) Saul's wife, and (2) David's wife. She was the mother of Amnon, whom Absalom slew.

Ahio: Son of Abinadab. He accompanied the ark to Jerusalem.

Ahithophel: The grandfather of Bathsheba. He was a respected advisor to David who defected to Absalom.

Amalekites: Residents of southern Judah who had bad relations with Israel until the time of David's reign.

Amasa: Absalom's general, slain by Joab.

Amnon: Son of David and Ahinoam. Sexually assaulted Tamar and was later killed by Absalom's servants.

Aphek: An important site on the coastal plain in Ephraim, near Ebenezer. Israel lost the ark here to the Philistines.

Arabah: Generally the desert; here a valley located north of the Dead Sea, surrounding the Jordan River.

Aroer: A site in Judah to which David sent a portion of the spoils taken from an Amalekite raid.

Ashdod: The Philistine city on the coastal plain to which the ark was taken following the Israelite defeat at Ebenezer.

Ashkelon: Philistine city, ten miles south of Ashdod.

Ashtaroth: The female Canaanite goddess; Baal's consort.

Baale-judah: Another name for Kiriath-jearim, where the ark rested following its return from the Philistines.

Baal-hazor: The site where Absalom conducted a sheep-shearing festival and Amnon was murdered.

Baal-perazim: A valley site west of Jerusalem where David defeated the Philistines.

Bahurim: A site near Jerusalem where Shimei cursed David as he fled Jerusalem.

Beeroth: A city in Benjamin territory from which came Rechab and Baanah, the assassins of Ishbosheth.

Beer-sheba: The major city in extreme southern Judah. Samuel's sons, Joel and Abijah, were judges here.

Benaiah: One of the famous leaders of David's army; he captained the Cherethites and the Pelethites.

Benjamin: Saul's home, a region slightly north of Jerusalem.

Bethel: A city in Israel lying between the territories of Benjamin and Ephraim which Samuel visited on his circuit as judge.

Beth-shan: A city at the entrance to the Valley of Jezreel. The Philistines hung the corpses of Saul and Jonathan here.

Beth-shemesh: A city in the north central section of Judah, to which the ark came first after leaving the Philistines.

Bezek: A city in northern Israel, where Saul assembled his army before rescuing Jabesh from the Ammonites.

Calebite: Descendants of Caleb, one of Joshua's spies. Caleb's family settled in southern Judah.

Carmel: (1) an important mountain on the northern coast of Israel; (2) a small village in Judah a few miles south of Hebron.

Cherethites: A group of foreign mercenary soldiers serving David. They may have come from the island of Crete.

Cherub (pl. *Cherubim*): A Canaanite mythological figure in the form of a winged bull. These figures were depicted (carved) atop the ark of the covenant.

Dagon: A Canaanite fertility god worshiped by the Philistines. His temple in Ashdod experienced unusual events following the capture of the Israelite ark.

Ebenezer: A site in Israel near Aphek where the Philistines defeated Israel and captured the ark.

Ekron: A Philistine city located on the southwestern coastal plain. The Philistines brought the ark here from Gath.

Eleazar: (1) a son of Abinadab who was placed in charge of the ark at Kiriath-jearaim; (2) one of the *three*, a group of David's select soldiers.

Elhanan: One of David's soldiers who slew a giant named Goliath.

Eli: The priest at Shiloh to whom Samuel was brought as an apprentice priest.

Elkanah: The father of Samuel.

Endor: Village in northern Israel where Saul consulted a medium.

Ephod: (1) A sacred garment worn by the priests, and (2) a box containing the sacred lots, Urim and Thummim.

Ephraim: A territory in Israel, north of Benjamin and south of Manasseh; important cities in this region were Shiloh, Bethel, and Ramathaim-zophim.

Gath: One of the five principal Philistine cities. Its king, Achish, accepted David as a mercenary soldier. A resident of Gath is known as a *Gittite*.

Geshur: Small kingdom south of Syria, located in Transjordan.

Gibeath-Elohim: The site in Benjaminite territory where Saul prophesied; may also be known as *Gibeah of Benjamin*.

Gibeon: A city located approximately five miles north of Jerusalem. The residents of this city suffered a massacre at the hands of Saul, for which the Lord sent a great famine until proper atonement could be made.

Gilboa: The mountain in northern Israel where Saul died.

Gilgal: An important religious center, located a mile or so east of Jericho. Saul was crowned here.

Girzites: A tribe of people living south of Jerusalem and Philistia. David raided their camps during his stay at Ziklag.

Gob: An unknown site where David fought two battles with the Philistines.

Hachilah: An unidentified site near Hebron or Ziph where David hid from Saul.

Hadadezer: The king of Zobah, in Syria, whom David defeated.

Hamath: The principal city in a region of southern Israel.

Hanun: The son of Nahash, king of the Ammonites. Hanun humiliated two of David's envoys and caused war with Israel.

Hannah: The mother of Samuel and the wife of Elkanah.

Hazor: A major city in northern Israel, approximately nine miles north of the Sea of Galilee.

Hebron: One of the principal cities in Judah, located approximately eleven miles south of Jerusalem. Hebron was David's first capital; Absalom's revolt began here.

Hiram: A tenth-century king of Tyre, a Phoenician city on the Mediterranean coast. Hiram is said to have supplied David with materials for work on the royal palace in Jerusalem.

Hophni: One of the two sons of Eli who assisted their father as priests at Shiloh. Because of his sins against the Lord, he died in the battle of Ebenezer-Aphek.

Hushai: One of David's faithful servants who played an important role in Absalom's unsuccessful revolt.

Ichabod: The son of Phinehas, Eli's son, whose name (*there is no glory*) reflected the sense of despair that hung over Israel following the Philistine capture of the ark.

Ishbosheth: The son of Saul who fled, with Abner, to Mahanaim and established a weak government in exile. His reign was as brief as it was ineffective.

Ittai: The Philistine mercenary soldier from Gath who served David in his fight against Absalom.

Jabesh-gilead: An important Israelite city in Gilead, a few miles east of the Jordan River. Saul rescued this city from the Ammonites in an act of great heroism.

Jabin: An important Canaanite king of Hazor whose army was defeated by Joshua during the conquest. This victory was cited by Samuel as evidence of God's saving acts for Israel.

Jebusites: The inhabitants of Jerusalem whom David defeated to gain control of the city. They were a Canaanite tribe.

Jedediah: An alternative name for Solomon, suggesting God's special affection for him and his father.

Jehoshaphat: A chief official in David's government, listed as the *recorder*. His exact responsibilities are unclear.

Jerubbabel: An alternative name given to Gideon the judge.

Jeshimon: A territory in Ziph, south of Hebron. David and his men hid close to this region during their days as renegades.

Jezreel: A major valley separating northern and southern Israel (Galilee from Samaria). Parts of this valley are often referred to as *Esdraelon*. Megiddo lay in this valley.

Joab: David's nephew; brother of Abishai and Asahel; commander of David's army. Joab was David's most loyal and astute servant, but also he was the most ruthless.

Jonadab: David's nephew, and a friend of Amnon. He helped Amnon devise a plan to seduce Tamar.

Jonathan: (1) The son of Saul who became close friends with David; he was also a valiant warrior. (2) The son of Abiathar, the priest; he aided David during Absalom's revolt.

Josheb-basshebeth: Leader of a special unit of David's army.

Kenites: A tribe residing in the southernmost regions of Judah, possibly in the Negeb area. They befriended the Israelites during the Exodus, and thus received favorable treatment from both Saul and David.

Kiriath-jearim: A small village in Judah, approximately nine miles west of Jerusalem. When the Philistines returned the ark, it remained here until David took it to Jerusalem.

Kish: The father of Saul; he belonged to the Matrite clan, from the tribe of Benjamin.

Mahanaim: Site of Ishbosheth's reign in exile over Israel; located in Gilead.

Maon: A region in Judah, south of Hebron, where David resided during his days as a refugee from Saul.

Mephibosheth: The name of Jonathan's son, to whom David extended care and compassion.

Merab: The eldest daughter of Saul. David sentenced five of her sons to death at the hands of the Gibeonites as expiation for Saul's bloodguilt.

Michal: The younger daughter of Saul who married David; later Saul gave her to Palti.

Mizpah, Mizpeh: An unidentified site in Moab, across from the Dead Sea. David carried his parents here for safety.

Moab: A kingdom located across from the Dead Sea in Transjordan; Moab played different roles in Israel's history, from ally to slave.

Nabal: A wealthy sheep owner from Judah, husband of Abigail.

Nahash: The king of the Ammonites; he attacked the city of Jabesh-gilead, but was defeated by Saul and his new army.

Nathan: David's court prophet. He announced God's word to David regarding the proposed temple. Also, he condemned David for the Bathsheba affair.

Negeb: A desert region lying south of Judah, extending to the Gulf of Aqabah.

Obed-edom: The person who tended the ark while God's anger abated from a mishandling of the sacred object. He was a Philistine from Gath.

Paran: A region far south of Hebron, north of the Negeb. David came here during his sojourn in Judah to try and escape Saul.

Pelethites: A group of foreign mercenaries who served as David's personal bodyguards, along with the Cherethites.

Peninnah: The wife of Elkanah in addition to Hannah. She taunted Hannah because she had no children.

Perez-uzzah: The name honoring the place where Uzzah died trying to move the ark from Baale-judah to Jerusalem.

Philistines: Aegean settlers along the coast of Palestine during the eleventh century; they challenged Israel for control of the central hill country of Ephraim.

Phinehas: The son of Eli, who served also as priest at Shiloh. He and Hophni, his brother, died in battle, carrying the ark.

Ramah: A village in Benjamin, about five miles north of Jerusalem, where Samuel resided as he judged Israel.

Ramathaim-zophim: The Ephraimite birthplace of Samuel.

Rechab: A Benjaminite soldier who, along with his brother, murdered Ishbosheth. David had both men killed for this deed.

Rephaim: A term used to identify a race of large people, or giants. Many gallant Israelites faced and defeated these giants.

Rimmon: The father of Rechab and Baanah, the assassins of Ishbosheth.

Rizpah: Saul's concubine who faithfully guarded the corpses of her sons who were hanged by the Gibeonites.

Seraiah: The secretary in David's court.

Shammah (also **Shimeab**): (1) David's brother, the father of Jonadab, Amnon's friend; he was also the father of Jonathan who killed a Philistine giant from Gath. (2) The third member of David's special unit known as the *three*. (3) The son of Harod, a member of another of David's special groups, the *thirty*.

Sheba: The son of Bichri; led a minor revolt against David.

Shiloh: A major cultic center in Ephraim, north of Bethel. Eli and his sons served as priests here.

Shimei: The Benjaminite who cursed David as he fled Jerusalem in the wake of Absalom's revolt.

Shunem: A site across from Mt. Gilboa where the Philistines camped to prepare for a battle with Saul and the Israelites.

Shur: A region in or southwest of the Negeb, bordering close to Egypt. David and Saul made raids as far south as Shur.

Tamar: The daughter of David and sister of Absalom. She was the victim of a brutal sexual assault by Amnon, her half-brother.

Toi: King of Hamath, a principality in Syria.

Tyre: An important Phoenician city, whose king, Hiram, supplied David with materials for his palace in Jerusalem.

Uzzah: A son of Abinadab, whose mishandling of the ark as it was being returned to Jerusalem led to his death.

Zeruiah: The mother of Joab, Abishai, and Asahel; she may have been a sister to David.

Ziba: The servant of Mephibosheth who cleverly managed to obtain half his master's estate.

Ziklag: A city in Judah, presented to David by Achish, king of Gath, as a royal grant.

Ziph: A wilderness in Judah, south of Hebron, where David hid during his days as a refugee.

Zobah: The Syrian province over which Hadadezer ruled.

Guide to Pronunciation

Abel-Beth-Maacah: AH-bell-BETH-mah-ah-CAH
Abiathar: Ah-bi-AH-thar
Abijah: Ah-BEE-juh
Abinadab: Ah-BIH-nuh-dab
Abishai: AA-bih-shigh
Achish: Ah-KEESH
Adonijah: Ah-doh-NIGH-juh
Adoram: Ah-DORE-um
Ahimaaz: Ah-HIH-mah-az
Ahimelech: Ah-HIH-meh-lek
Ahinoam: Ah-hee-NOH-um
Ahithophel: Ah-HEE-thoh-fell
Aiah: Ah-EE-ah
Amasa: Ah-MAH-suh
Aphiah: Ah-FEE-ah
Arabah: AR-ah-bah
Armoni: Ar-MOH-nee
Aroer: Ah-ROH-er
Baale-judah: Bah-AHL-le-joo-DAH
Baal-hazor: Bah-AHL-hah-TSORE
Baal-perazim: Bah-AHL-per-rah-ZEEM
Baanah: Bah-ah-NAH
Bahurim: Bah-hoo-REEM
Becorath: Beh-COR-rath
Beeroth: Buh-eh-ROTHE
Benaiah: Beh-NIGH-uh
Berothai: Beh-roh-THAI
Besor: Beh-SORE
Bezek: BAY-zek
Cherethites: CHAIR-uh-thites
Chileab: CHIH-lee-ab
Dagon: DAY-gone
Eleazar: Ell-ee-AY-zar

Elhanan: ELL-hah-non
Eliada: Ell-lee-AH-dah
Elishama: Ell-lee-SHAH-mah
Elishua: Ell-lee-SHOO-ah
Elkanah: ELL-kah-nah
Ephod: EE-fod
Eshtemoa: Esh-teh-MOH-ah
Gallim: Gal-LEEM
Gibeath-Elohim: GIB-ee-ath-el-oh-HEEM
Hachilah: Hah-kee-LAH
Hadadezer: Hah-dah-DAY-zer
Hamath: Hah-MAHTH
Hanun: HAH-nun
Hazor: HAH-tsore
Hushai: HOO-shigh
Ibhar: IB-har
Ishbi-benob: ISH-bee-BAY-nob
Ishbosheth: ISH-boh-sheth
Ithream: ITH-ree-um
Jabesh-gilead: JAH-besh-GIH-lee-ad
Jabin: Jah-BEAN
Japhia: Jah-PHEE-ah
Jebushites: JEB-you-sites
Jedediah: Jeh-deh-DIGH-uh
Jehoshaphat: Jeh-HOH-shuh-fat
Jerahmeelites: Jeh-RAH-meh-uh-lites
Jerubaal: Jeh-ROO-buh-all
Jeshanah: JESH-ah-nah
Jeshimon: Jeh-SHEE-mun
Jonadab: JOH-nuh-dab
Josheb-basshebeth: JOH-sheh-bah-SHAY-beth
Kiriath-jearim: KIR-ree-ath-jeh-uh-REEM
Laish: Lah-EESH
Machir: Mah-KEER
Mahanaim: Mah-hah-NAY-yim
Malchishua: Mahl-kee-SHOO-uh
Maon: Mah-OWN
Matrites: MAH-trites

Mephibosheth: Meh-FIH-boh-sheth
Merab: MARE-ab
Michal: Mee-KAHL
Mizpah, Mispeh: MIZZ-puh
Nabal: Nah-BALL
Nacon: Nah-CONE
Nahash: Nah-HASH
Obed-edom: OH-bed-EE-dum
Paran: Pah-RAHN
Pelethites: PEH-leh-thites
Peninnah: Peh-NEE-nah
Perez-uzzah: PEH-rez-OO-zah
Phinehas: Fih-NAY-has
Ramathaim-zophim: Rah-mah-THAH-eem-zoh-FEEM
Rechab: Reh-KAHB
Rehob: RAY-hob
Rephaim: Reh-fah-YEEM
Rizpah: RIZ-pah
Seraiah: Ser-EYE-uh
Shaalim: Shah-ah-LEEM
Shalishah: Shah-lee-SHAH
Shammah: Shah-MAH
Shammua: Shah-MOO-ah
Shephatiah: Sheh-fah-TEE-ah
Shimeah: Shih-MAY-ah
Shimei: SHIH-migh
Shunem: SHOO-nem
Talmai: TAL-mai
Tamar: Tah-MAR
Uzzah: OO-zah
Zelzah: ZEL-zah
Zeror: Ze-ROAR
Zeruiah: Zeh-roo-EYE-ah
Ziba: ZEE-buh
Zobah: ZOH-bah

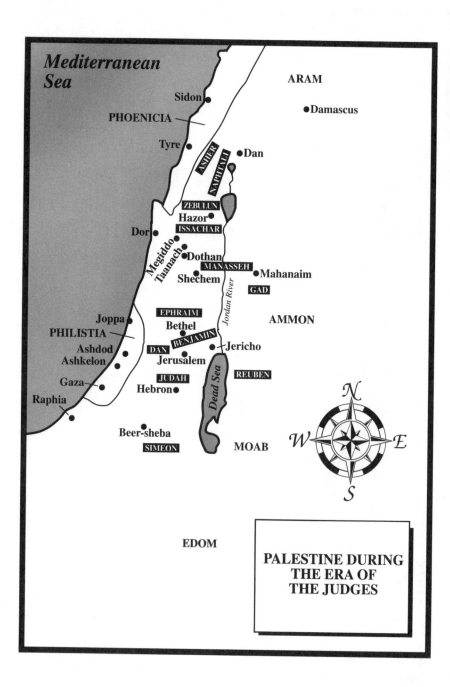

Mediterranean Sea

ARAM

Sidon

•Damascus

PHOENICIA

Tyre

ASHER

NAPHTALI

•Dan

ZEBULUN

Hazor•

ISSACHAR

Dor•

Megiddo•

Taanach•

•Dothan

MANASSEH

Shechem•

•Mahanaim

GAD

Jordan River

EPHRAIM

Joppa•

Bethel•

BENJAMIN

AMMON

PHILISTIA

DAN

•Jericho

Ashdod•

Jerusalem•

Ashkelon•

JUDAH

REUBEN

Gaza•

Hebron•

Raphia•

Dead Sea

Beer-sheba•

SIMEON

MOAB

N

W   E

S

EDOM

PALESTINE DURING
THE ERA OF
THE JUDGES

HITTITES

Ugarit

KITTIM
(Cyprus)

The
Great
Sea

Arvad

Hamath

Gebal

PHOENICIA

Sidon

Damascus

SYRIAN
DESERT

Tyre

Dan

Mt. Carmel

Megiddo

ISRAEL

AMMON

Joppa

Bethel

Jerusalem

PHILISTIA

Jericho

Ashdod

Gaza

Hebron

JUDAH

Raphia

MOAB

Beer-sheba

EDOM

THE KINGDOM OF
DAVID AND SOLOMON

—— Greatest extent of
the empire

▨ Territory conquered
by David

- - - Territory under economic
influence of Solomon

Ezion-geber